LET GO

Also by Hugh van Cuylenburg

The Resilience Project

THE RESILIENCE PROJECT

LET GO

HUGH VAN CUYLENBURG

LIFE

PENGUIN LIFE

UK | USA | Canada | Ireland | Australia
India | New Zealand | South Africa | China

Penguin Life is part of the Penguin Random House group of companies
whose addresses can be found at global.penguinrandomhouse.com

First published by Penguin Life in 2021

Cover design by Alex Ross © Penguin Random House Australia Pty Ltd
Author photograph on back cover by Tim Caraffa
Typeset in 13/18.5 pt Adobe Garamond by Midland Typesetters, Australia

Printed and bound in Australia by Griffin Press, part of Ovato, an accredited
ISO AS/NZS 14001 Environmental Management Systems printer

 A catalogue record for this
book is available from the
National Library of Australia

ISBN 978 1 76104 327 7

penguin.com.au

I would like to acknowledge the traditional custodians and storytellers of the lands on which I live and work. I pay my respects to all Elders, past and present.

To my beautiful children, Benji and Elsie. I love you more than you will ever know. May this book find its way into your hands when you need it most.

P.S. Please don't read Chapter 4.

CONTENTS

Fear of failure

Social media

Ego

AUTHOR'S NOTE

The world has changed since my last book, and so have I.

I have learnt more about resilience in the past two years than I have in my 41 years on earth.

The Resilience Project, my first book, was the culmination of a decade's work. Ten years spent researching the book's three central principles – gratitude, empathy and mindfulness – and presenting their benefits to audiences all over Australia and New Zealand.

Let Go, however, is different.

As I came across the topics that appear in the following pages, I knew I couldn't wait another ten years to write about them, so I'm proud to say the words in this book come from a place of humility and curiosity. I should point out that I'm not a psychologist, I am not a psychiatrist and I'm most certainly not a motivational speaker. I am a proud teacher and a storyteller.

Please also note that no wheels have been reinvented in the writing of this book. I am not the one who has discovered these topics. I am merely attempting to shine a light on some of the incredible work done by researchers across the globe; work which has helped me in my own journey.

One of my dearest friends, Al, an electrician by trade and one of the manliest men you will ever meet, recently said to me that the story about my sister overcoming an eating disorder in my first book gave him 'sweaty eyes'. I was confused for a while until I realised he was telling me (in manly words) that it made him cry.

I hope that in sharing my stories – some of which will make you laugh, some of which will give you sweaty eyes – you will discover new ways in which to feel happier and cope better in these challenging times.

There are so many wonderful books out there, and it means a lot to me that you have chosen to read this one.

A warning: *Let Go* contains material that deals with mental illness, sexual abuse and suicide. This may be triggering for some readers. For that reason, crisis support services are listed at the back and I would urge anyone facing mental health issues to contact a GP or mental health practitioner.

With gratitude,
Hugh van Cuylenburg

INTRODUCTION

For the longest time I've felt under intense pressure to 'be okay'.

It wasn't always this way. Growing up in Melbourne in the 1980s, I hadn't a worry in the world. *Everything* was okay. In fact, I didn't know what *not being okay* even looked like. My life was full of joy.

With no internet and no wireless gadgetry to lull me into a pixelated stupor, I knew all about boredom. And what an absolute blessing that was. If I wanted to vanquish the ennui of a dreary afternoon I had to get creative. My brother and sister and our childhood friends would all be drafted into the battle against tedium; games were invented and played, risks were taken and relationships were cemented.

On Saturday nights my family piled onto our small couch

to watch *Hey Hey It's Saturday*. On Sunday nights we'd do it again for *The Comedy Company*. Apart from the occasional treat of watching an ODI cricket match with my dad, that was my TV diet – two hours a week with the family, laughing together and connecting. The television had four thinly stocked channels and the phenomenon of reality TV was still two decades away over the cultural horizon.

On weeknights there was no social media platform in my room to erode my self-esteem. I never compared myself to others, or thought I wasn't popular or cool enough (insert your own shame story here). I believed that just being me was enough. I felt worthy of love and that I belonged. I felt . . . very okay.

Then, one day, everything changed.

Most of us can recall the first time we saw our parents cry. For a child it can be unnerving: the inadvertent slip of our protectors' tightly guarded secret that we're not as safe in the world as we think. I'll never forget the sad figure of my dad hunched over at the kitchen sink, sobbing as he washed the dishes. Mum had her arm around him as tears ran down her cheeks, too. My little sister Georgia had stopped eating at the age of fourteen as a result of mental illness. Those parental tears heralded the first time I realised that things could actually be not okay.

As the catastrophe engulfed our family, Mum and Dad invested their every effort in Georgia's recovery. They told themselves it was their responsibility to make sure she got better. Meanwhile, I was having a different inner conversation – a toxic and foolhardy one. I told myself that I had to be okay.

In fact, I believed I had to be *more* than okay. I felt as though I had to be a constant source of joy to everyone around me. With a potentially lethal health crisis unfolding in our household, I didn't dare add to the anguish by airing my own adolescent insecurities and fears.

Ultimately, Georgia recovered from anorexia but, for my part, I never quite came through the other side. I continued to cling to the belief that I had to make everyone I met feel happy. Always and at all costs.

While this, in part, led me to my life's purpose and the formation of The Resilience Project, at so many points, this self-imposed expectation was my undoing.

In 2020, the need to be okay had swelled into a giant, cresting wave. As COVID-19 death and infection rates skyrocketed around the world, and lockdowns strangled economies, communities and the human spirit, I was one of the people telling everyone how to cope. In radio interview after radio interview, TV appearance after TV appearance,

I offered advice on how to stay positive and emotionally strong in the face of a deadly worldwide plague.

Then, without warning, the giant wave broke on top of me.

On a cold Melbourne morning, during one of our many lockdowns, I was asked on live radio if I was okay.

'No, I'm not,' I blurted with unexpected candour. 'I'm totally and utterly broken.'

The answer shocked me more than anyone else. After the interview I walked back into the battle zone (my house) and realised I needed to make some big changes. I was a long way from being okay and had just admitted this on radio to tens of thousands of people.

After a decade spent telling people around the country we should all be seeing a mental health specialist, I heeded my own advice. A few weeks later – and for the first time in my life – I started seeing a great psychologist named Anita.

During one of our sessions, Anita said something to me that I will never ever forget. 'There comes a time in life, Hugh, when you realise you don't need to carry the events of your past around with you anymore. It's time for you to let go.'

Two little words – let go – landed on me with such weight that I shifted my chair back, leant forward and dropped my head into my hands. I stayed in that position for an intense couple of minutes. I knew instantly that Anita was right, but where was I supposed to begin? What, exactly, did I need to let go of? And once I found the answer to that, how exactly was I meant to let go? Unfortunately, Anita couldn't give me those answers. It took a lot of hard work and the best part of a year digging down within myself to work out what I had to do.

It turns out there were *a lot* of things I needed to let go of. I kept a journal by my side during the sessions with Anita. Every time we uncovered something that was holding me back, I would scribble it down. Before long, it started to read like a very embarrassing laundry list:

- Shame
- Expectation
- Perfection
- Control
- Fear of failure
- Ego.

Each night, after my wife Penny and the kids had gone to bed, I would get out my journal and stare at the list. I would then think back over my life and attach examples and stories to the entries, so I would both remember and understand their significance. As I closed the journal one night, I decided to hide it in a drawer. Imagine if someone found it? What a disaster that would be. *No one* can ever read this, I thought to myself.

As the months wore on and the COVID-19 situation worsened, it became obvious that I wasn't the only one suffering from the sorts of issues that were on my list. In fact, the more I explored them, the more I realised they lay at the heart of much of society's collective and individual unhappiness.

Before too long, I concluded that *everyone* needed to hear this stuff. *Everyone* could benefit from knowing what was in my journal! In fact, I started to feel the exact same way I did, thirteen years before, when I'd been lucky enough to witness a Himalayan desert community practising gratitude, empathy and mindfulness.

I hope that in sharing my embarrassing 'laundry list' I can encourage you to let go too and embrace a different way of thinking and living.

Before we begin, though, there's something important you need to do: you need to be prepared to make yourself vulnerable. You need to lean in and see vulnerability for what it truly is – a superpower. Because before you can let go of shame, expectation, control, perfection, ego, fear of failure, or whatever it is that's holding you back, you have to let down your guard. You have to be prepared to be vulnerable.

From a psychological point of view, vulnerability is simply the ability to take an emotional risk. This may sound counterintuitive. After all, one of our most basic human instincts is to avoid harm. We spend much of our time scanning the terrain for physical and psychological threats, and plotting a course – often subconsciously – to get us to the end of another day unscathed.

This hardwired instinct for self-preservation is a great thing during risky activities like driving a car or cooking with gas. But when it comes to fostering relationships, deepening interpersonal connections or managing our mental health, dancing around the danger or curling up in an emotionally defensive ball only leaves us even *more* wounded.

In many cultures – most definitely in Australia – people are primed from a young age to 'save face' or 'harden up' when confronted with threats to our sense of mental security. We're supposed to be tough when we feel emotions like shame, guilt and embarrassment. This is particularly true among males. After all, 'boys don't cry', right?

I know this only too well. I spent much of my life avoiding any kind of exposure to harm – whether it was physical or mental. This might go some way to explaining why, as a cricketer, I was always so hopeless with the bat. It also explains my obsession with trying to make everyone feel happy all the time.

Try as we might, we cannot avoid psychological hardship. Nor can we avoid the chaos of modern life as it detonates all around us. Unhappiness and emotional discomfort are important parts of our journey. It's what we do when they arise that truly counts.

After I began the sessions with Anita in 2020, I spent a lot of time looking back over my life, as you tend to do when you're in therapy. Pondering the definition of vulnerability one day, I reflected on a remarkable person I once met.

At the end of the launch of my first book in Melbourne back in 2019, I was sitting at a table, signing copies, when I was approached by a middle-aged lady. She was with a group of young adults but as she came towards me she turned to them and said, 'You guys wait here.'

'I just had my last round of chemo today,' she said when we were alone. 'I've only got a few months left. I've driven two hours to get here tonight and brought my three kids and their partners along. Would you please sign these books for them and tell them how much I love them?'

I had to fight the impulse to cry.

'I've bored my kids with your resilience, gratitude and empathy stuff for ages,' she went on, smiling. 'I needed them to come along tonight because this is what's going to get them through the next few years.'

So I did what this courageous and beautiful mum asked me to. I took a pen and wrote to her children that she loved them more than words could ever express. Then I stood up and wrapped my arms around her frail frame. Our hug was long and silent. And then she was gone.

It was one of the most memorable encounters of my life. The vulnerability this woman showed in those few minutes will stay with me forever. I don't even know her name, but I'll never forget her.

All of the stories in this book concern human vulnerability in one form or another. I have taken them directly from my journal and placed them here as jumping-off points to explore deeper emotional waters, where, all too often, we become snagged by unhelpful thoughts, feelings and behaviours that hold us back from being okay.

So, it's time to begin. It's time to let go.

SHAME

CHAPTER 1
DEAR GEORGIA, TAKE TWO

For my little sister, Georgia. I am sorry I was unable to protect you, and that I wasn't there for you years later when you needed me most.

The dedication above, which I wrote and placed at the start of *The Resilience Project*, had an unexpected consequence: literally thousands of people made the effort to get in touch. Most wanted to reassure me that I *couldn't* have protected Georgia.

'You shouldn't beat yourself up,' they wrote.

'It wasn't your fault.'

'You were too young.'

When I was six and Georgia was three, a stranger came into the front yard of my grandparents' house where we were playing. He picked up my sister and carried her around the side of the house. Then he sexually assaulted her.

Georgia didn't tell anyone what happened and carried the horrible secret throughout her childhood. At the age of 14 she developed anorexia nervosa. When that cloud descended on our family I dealt with it by scoffing at the diagnosis ('All she has to do is eat!') and removing myself from the picture so I could spend as much time as possible at my girlfriend's house.

In 2019, when *The Resilience Project* was published, readers forgave me for this as well.

'You were only eighteen and in love for the first time,' they pointed out.

'It's only natural you wanted to live the life of a normal young man.'

Their kind words meant a lot to me because it had taken years to come to terms with the shame I felt for abandoning my little sister. It's also taken years for me to forgive myself for not doing more for her when I was six. I now look at my young son playing with his little sister, and know deep in my heart that I could not have protected Georgia from that paedophile when we were kids.

There's something else, however, that I've found hard to forgive myself for and for which I feel deep shame. It is, in fact, the real reason I wrote the dedication; something that I wasn't ready to write about in my first book, something that happened much later.

In 2009, Georgia flew home from her new base in Los Angeles and called a family meeting. As we gathered at our parents' house, my sister finally revealed, after twenty-three years, what had happened to her that afternoon at our grandparents' house. During sessions with a therapist, she had unearthed the deeply buried sexual trauma. As she recounted the events of that day, my blood ran cold.

The second Georgia described a man coming into our grandparents' yard I remembered it, too. I pictured him walking into the garden and first trying to talk to me. When I didn't respond I saw him pick up Georgia and carry her around the side of the house. I had no idea what happened next.

As Georgia spoke to us that night I could tell she was broken. My sister was the most vulnerable I had ever seen her, which is saying a lot. When she looked at me with pain and sorrow in her eyes I knew exactly what I had to do: I needed to give her a big hug and say, 'I was there with you that day. I remember that man. It was real. You are not crazy. I know it happened. Keep going. I'm here for you.'

Instead, I stayed silent.

For reasons I don't really understand I just couldn't form the words that might have helped my sister. I knew I was fucking up in real time. Jesus Christ! She needs you right now, I berated myself. You could give her so much strength and support in this moment.

Instead, I let her flounder through one of the hardest moments of her life.

'I'm really sorry that happened to you,' was all I could manage.

With every second that passed I knew I was drifting further from Georgia – and from any chance of throwing her a lifeline. The longer my lips remained sealed, the more I floated off towards some distant emotional horizon. Mum and Dad and my younger brother Josh, on the other hand, rallied around Georgia and responded from the heart.

'Darling, you've done so well to get to where you are after what was done to you.'

'Thank you for telling us.'

'This makes so much sense of the journey you've been on.'

'We are all here for you.'

'You're strong. You're amazing. You're beautiful.'

'I'm proud of you.'

I was sitting right there with them but I was as remote as an orbiting moon. My pitiful offering – 'I'm really sorry that happened to you' – hung like a weight around my neck. Much later it would start to choke me. Had I chosen to validate Georgia and walk beside her, we might have formed an unbreakable bond. It might have changed both of our lives in the best possible way.

A couple of days later, Georgia returned to the US, no doubt with a little weight lifted off her shoulders, thanks to my loving family. I went back to my life with a crushing shame pressing down hard on mine. I tried not to think about my emotional betrayal but whenever I did, I realised the sexual assault had ultimately led to us *both* feeling ashamed. I couldn't blame the predator for all of it. After all, I could have done or said something to help – any time I wanted.

Whenever I thought about doing or saying the right thing, though, I always fell back on selfish excuses for not doing so – the same excuses that had stopped me from speaking on that day at Mum and Dad's: it was too messy; it would make me too vulnerable; it would be too painful to admit after all this time and, in a way, it would probably hurt Georgia again, too. It was easier shoving my shame back in a box rather than engaging with it, so I put it off and put it off and put it off again – for ten years.

■

In 2019, it was finally time to face the ugly truth. Georgia was still living in Los Angeles and I had sent her the first chapter of my book to make sure she was okay with it, since it was about her. This got us talking about our relationship. They were just baby steps, but progress, nonetheless.

As I was finishing the last chapter of the book, I knew the time had come. Dread swelled in my chest as I messaged Georgia to arrange a time to chat. It was the first hot day of spring. Normally I love balmy weather: when the mercury pushes into the high 20s and beyond my mood goes along for the ride. On this day, however, the heat was suffocating and just magnified the emotions of what I was about to do. I felt sick.

When Georgia answered the phone, I headed outside and sat down beneath a big gum tree in our backyard. There was something comforting about that towering eucalypt: it reminded me of our childhood backyard which was anchored by eight of these enormous trees. I rested my back against the tree trunk, my knees pulled up and my head hung low.

'I'm so sorry,' I began, and then I read her the dedication I had written.

'Gee, that's so silly,' she said gently, aware I was not my usual self. 'You couldn't have protected me from what happened that day.'

'I'm not talking about that day,' I said. 'I'm talking about twenty years later, at Mum and Dad's, when you told us all what happened.'

'What do you mean?' she asked.

'Well . . . I remembered that day at our grandparents', too,' I said softly. 'The yard, the man; that he picked you up and took you around the side of the house. As soon as you told us about it, I remembered it straight away. I had no idea what had happened to you when the man took you away, but I did clearly remember him opening the front gate and walking towards us. I'm so sorry.'

Georgia was silent for a long time. I imagined she was poring over the catalogue of memories from her painful 33-year journey as a survivor of child sexual abuse. I could sense her demeanour change from confused to sad and disappointed as the gravity of what I had just said sank in. If only I'd spoken out and helped her ten years earlier, she might have been able to make more progress towards inner peace.

As sunlight streamed through the leaves of the gum tree overhead, I stared hard at my phone, holding it out in front of my face, on speaker mode. It felt like we had arrived at a crossroads in our relationship.

'I've been wanting to have a conversation like this with you for so many years,' Georgia began. 'You know, a *real* conversation about real things and real feelings. So thank you for being real today.'

For all my sense of dread, I should have known which road my compassionate and resilient little sister would take. She wasn't angry or judgemental. Sad and frustrated? Yes. But more than anything she seemed relieved.

For years Georgia had watched from afar as my work with The Resilience Project gathered momentum. I think she found it hard reconciling the vulnerable and empathetic man she heard about in the media with her somewhat aloof big brother.

Whenever I had a few spare minutes in the car, I would phone a couple of go-to friends, just to say, 'G'day, how are you going?' No pressure to have a great conversation; no need to wrestle with the mysteries of life – just a quick dose of love to fill in the cracks of a busy day.

My sister Georgia was never one of the people I called.

Today she is.

I look back at those ten lost years with enormous regret because the shame I felt put a huge amount of distance between us. Over time I have come to understand that this doesn't make me a bad person, it only makes me human.

Shame – and its close cousin guilt – are innate parts of being human. Shame is a universal emotion but unlike other feelings such as anger, joy and sorrow, the very personal nature of shame makes it virtually impossible for others to see, even those who are closest to us. Joy, fear, sadness, anger, disgust? These types of feelings are worn on the sleeve, out on display to be shared and processed with others. More often than not, shame is a table set for one.

SHAME VS GUILT

The distinction between shame and guilt can be expressed like this: guilt is feeling bad about what you *did*, shame is feeling bad about who you *are*. Shame is the emotion of self-disappointment; a reaction to aspects of our inner lives we are so embarrassed by that we instinctively conceal them from the world. In short, shame is the stuff we hide and it makes *us* hide too – the opposite of human connection. Just consider the distance it had put between my sister and me.

Like embarrassment and guilt, shame is regarded as a 'moral emotion'. American professor of psychology June Tangney has written widely on shame and says it functions as an 'emotional moral barometer'. In other words, shame gives

us immediate feedback on our social and moral acceptabil-
ity. 'When we sin, transgress, or err,' says Professor Tangney,
'aversive feelings of shame, guilt, or embarrassment are likely
to ensue.'[1]

That doesn't mean shame is always a bad thing.
Reminding ourselves when and where we make mistakes
usually means we'll be equipped to make better decisions
in the future. By guiding us towards more acceptable social
behaviour, shame not only helps us as individuals, it helps
the wider community, too.

Paradoxically, there is both *healthy* shame and *unhealthy*
shame. The difference lies in the reasons *why* we feel ashamed
and how we choose to respond to it. Since shame is such a
private emotion – even a secret one – there are no checks and
balances, like the perspective of a loved one or friend, to pre-
vent it from turning toxic. To quote Oprah Winfrey, 'We all
tell ourselves unkind and mostly untrue stories about ourselves, and then marinate in those stories our entire lives.'

Don't we know it? There are as many reasons to feel
shame as there are people on the planet. Not all of them are
tied to poor behaviour or bad choices, like my failure to help
Georgia in a time of need. Often shame stems from feelings
of inadequacy, perceived weaknesses or character flaws – the
key ingredients in the poisonous 'marinade' Oprah Winfrey

is referring to. Negative self-talk arises when we compare ourselves to others or hear criticism from someone else. Here are a few common 'shame stories':

- I'm not good-looking enough.
- I'm not smart enough.
- I'm going bald so I'll never have a girlfriend.
- I have bulbous eyes so if a girl manages to get past the hair situation, she'll *definitely* draw the line at the eyeballs.

Okay, so I may have gone straight to my own shame stories but hopefully they're relatable examples of the harmful things we all tell ourselves. And make no mistake, they *are* harmful.

The effects of shame and guilt have long been clinically linked with all sorts of psychological problems, from depression and anxiety to bipolar, schizophrenia, substance abuse and eating disorders.[2] Not to mention the consequences for our self-esteem and our relationships. As American self-help author Mark Manson bluntly puts it, 'Shame can fuck us up.'[3] And it can do so for a very long time: I've carried shame stories with me since I was in primary school (I'll come to them later).

Obviously, it's the *unhealthy* shame – the type that holds us back as opposed to that which encourages higher moral goals – that we need to let go of. But how? My psychologist Anita helped me understand how by suggesting I use a simple three-step process.

Before I go on, I know that not everyone has access to a psychologist, particularly since COVID-19 triggered a mental health epidemic. Thankfully, the three-step process can also be undertaken with the help of a counsellor, a social worker, a therapist or an occupational therapist, to name but a few. If you are not fortunate enough to have a professional to guide you, I'll give you some examples of how letting go of shame could look, using my own shame story. As you're no doubt discovering, there are many such stories that I allowed to poison my relationship with my sister, but here I will focus on just one:

I abandoned Georgia when she was sick and needed me most

Step 1: Separate who *you are* from *what you did*

We all stuff up from time to time, sometimes quite badly. Unfortunately, in the wake of stuff-ups we often then tell ourselves we are bad people. When this feeling arises it is vital we remind ourselves, '*I* am not bad. What I *did* was bad.'

For decades I told myself I was a bad brother and a bad son for not hanging around much after Georgia got sick. Instead of staying home and helping however I could, I was off at my girlfriend's. I wasn't a bad person: I just made a bad decision. That's something we all do. It's part of life. It is also part of life to learn from our bad decisions and aim to do better next time.

Step 2: Empathise with the *real* motivation behind your actions

There's always motivation behind the choices we make. Often they are obvious; sometimes they bubble up from deep in our subconscious. Too often we don't bother trying to understand why we act in certain ways or question the motives.

The underlying motive for my behaviour when Georgia was sick stemmed from the stage of life I was in:

- I was 18.
- I had just finished school.
- I had just got my driver's licence.
- I had just fallen in love for the first time.

Faced with the choice of being home, where Georgia's condition was an ongoing source of grief, or going to my girlfriend Christie's house, or the pub, or the cricket, or the football . . . for a young man it was no choice at all. Now that I'm in my forties, I can empathise with that young man. Furthermore, I forgive him. I was 18 and just wanted to feel happy – an understandable motive for my behaviour.

Step 3: Share your shame

Now, this is the hard part. It feels counterintuitive but, as US professor and author Brené Brown says, 'Shame cannot survive being spoken [because] it cannot survive empathy.'[4] What Brené Brown means is that when you open up and tell your story from the heart (and to the right person) it will almost always be met with love, support and empathy.

In an ideal world we would share our shame with a therapist, but you don't have to know a trained professional. You do, however, need someone who will show you love, support and empathy. Be picky about who you share your shame with. Not everyone has earnt the right to hear it. You will know those people instinctively: they're the ones who will say things like, 'I'm here for you.' Or, 'I know what that feels like.' Or, 'I've also stuffed up before.'

Before I told Anita my shame story about abandoning Georgia when she was sick, the only other person I'd confided in was one of my best mates, Collo. Collo is not a trained professional and he wasn't sitting on a therapist's couch taking notes on a clipboard: Collo works for a pharmaceutical company, and I was sobbing into a chicken souvlaki as we sat on the roadside together having drunk countless beers at the cricket.

Despite nursing a putrid hangover the next day, I felt bloody fantastic. I doubt he knows it, but by allowing me to expose my shame, Collo's warmth was the beginning of the end of a period of mental anguish. When I reflect on it now, his empathy that night gave me the confidence to share the shame again, this time with Anita.

I know I'm not a special case: we all harbour shame stories. Some are minor while some go much deeper and hold us back or force us to hide. As Mark Manson says, 'It's the *hiding* of ourselves, *not the shame itself*, that fucks us all up psychologically.'[5]

Whatever shame stories you're telling yourself, it's time to stop hiding them. Separate them from who you are, empathise with them and then share them. Only then will you be able to let them go.

CHAPTER 2
SHOW-AND-TELL

Back in 1988, Fridays in Mrs Bewley's Year 2 class at Greythorn Primary School were the best. Not because it meant the weekend was close, but because Friday was our 'show-and-tell' day. Alongside PE, it was my favourite time.

For those of you unfamiliar with 'show-and-tell', kids are asked to bring in a random object from home. It could be a toy. Or a piece of sporting equipment. Sometimes even something inanimate, like a story. Anyway, you stand up the front of the class and *show* whatever it is you've brought in. Then you *tell* them all about it. Simple. Once the showing and telling are done, the rules state that the class must ask you three questions. Without fail, the questions in Mrs Bewley's class were always, 'Do you like it?', 'Who gave it to you?' and 'Where do you keep it?'

One of my best mates back in Year 2 was a kid called Andrew Crawford. He made me laugh so hard. One of his best gags was asking the 'show and tell' question that made the *least* amount of sense. A popular girl named Greta Thraves once regaled us with a story about her family's planned holiday to Queensland. As she scanned the audience for questions, Andrew's hand shot up. 'Yes, Andrew?' Greta asked. 'Where do you keep it?' Andrew said. As an eight-year-old, that really tickled me. On another occasion, a shy boy named Justin told us he'd won a big race on the weekend. 'Who gave it to you?' Andrew inquired. Brilliant!

Mrs Bewley's rotating roster meant we took turns bringing in artefacts from home and bragging to the class about how good they were. There were no restrictions – we could turn up with whatever we liked. In 1988, my eighth birthday fell on a Monday, which triggered the longest week of my young life. I was one of the four names on the show-and-tell roster that Friday but that meant waiting *four whole days* before I could dazzle everyone with the birthday presents I'd received. When you're eight, four days is like four years.

When show-and-tell Friday finally rolled around, Mrs Bewley called our names and up we went to the front of the classroom. I made sure I'd go last because I knew my items were going to blow people's minds. As a selfless Year 2 student, I remember thinking it wouldn't be fair to make someone follow me. It was wiser to save the best until last and finish with a bang.

In one hand I held a spinning top that came alive with coloured flashing lights and a weird whirring sound. Although I considered it a must-see for my classmates, it was only the curtain-raiser. The main event, which I tried to hold behind my back, was my brand-new AFL Sherrin football. When Mum and Dad presented me with it on Monday morning it instantly became my most treasured possession.

I polished the Sherrin with dubbin to waterproof the glistening red leather and kept it at the end of my bed. Knowing show-and-tell was coming up I decided I wouldn't use it until the weekend because I was convinced everyone at school would want to see it in its pristine, unblemished condition. Now, as I stood at the back of the queue and waited for my big moment, I realised that showing off the Sherrin wasn't the only thing I was busting to do. After a solid session on the water bubbler at recess, I needed to wee.

I was in a bit of a pickle because if I left the classroom everyone would see what was hidden behind my back. I decided to tough it out. Thankfully the first two kids did the right thing and spoke pretty quickly: they showed their items, fielded some questions, everybody clapped and then they sat down.

Good, I thought. I'm going to make it.

Next up was Natasha. I'll never forget her because she was Kylie Minogue's little sister. Or at least she claimed to be. Whenever Natasha was challenged – on the basis she had a different surname to the pop superstar – she responded with the iron-clad, no-need-for-further-debate rebuke, 'Ask my mum!'

Natasha didn't big-note about her world-famous sibling at show-and-tell on this particular day. Instead, Natasha wanted to talk about her book of pressed flowers. Good – this will be pretty quick, too, I thought. By this stage, the pressure on my bladder was pushing into the red zone. Natasha was extremely proud of her pressed flowers, however, and she went to great pains to show the class every single one that had been lovingly squished into her book.

As Natasha finally concluded her great botanical boast and sat down amid resounding applause, I knew I was in trouble. *Big* trouble. The spotlight fell squarely on me.

Clutching my spinning top (not a euphemism) and trying to keep the Sherrin hidden behind me, I knew the show must go on. After all, I was the headline act.

'Good afternoon, Mrs Bewley. Good afternoon Year 2,' I began in a trembling soprano. By this point, I'd developed a headache from holding on for so long and I couldn't recall a word of the two-part presentation I'd spent the whole week rehearsing. 'Today I . . .' I squeezed my eyes shut and willed every cell in my body to stop it from happening. 'Today, I . . . I'm, I'm going to show you . . .'

The next sound in class 2B was the eruption of screams from twenty-odd children – all aghast as the hot gush darkened the fabric of my tracksuit pants and made its way south before pooling in my sandals and spilling onto the floor.

There's an old adage among primary schoolteachers about the things that always lead to chaos. Number one is a dog in the school grounds at lunchtime. Number two is a bird trapped in the classroom. But if you haven't seen a kid wet his pants in front of the entire class then you don't know what chaos is. It was worse than a bird *and* a dog trapped in the classroom.

Almost all of the kids had leapt to their feet and were running around, shrieking at the top of their lungs. Not running for the door, mind you – just running at random tangents and pinballing off one another as they tried to get as far away as possible from me. 'Do you like it?' Andrew Crawford yelled at the top of his lungs.

It's kind of interesting that I would go on to make a living as a public speaker because, even as screams filled the air and urine filled my sandals, I tried to stay on message. 'Today I want to show you this great spinning top,' I said sobbing but still managing to hold the top aloft. 'And I also brought my brand-new . . .'

At this point Mrs Bewley cut in. She gently put her hand on my shoulder and suggested I call it a day. 'Come on, Hugh, let's get you cleaned up.' She escorted me to the toilet block where I sat hunched in a ball on the floor. How could I ever go back into that classroom? Would anyone still be my friend?

Worst of all, in 1988 I was madly in love with a girl named Veronica Hatfield. She'd been one of the first to start screaming and running in circles. My dreams of living happily ever after with Veronica were now washed away by a tide of you-know-what.

'Hugh, are you okay in there?' Mrs Bewley called from outside.

'No. I think I want my mum,' I squeaked.

That phone call had already been made and, ten minutes later, the next voice I heard was Mum's. She'd collected my schoolbag and brought a change of clothes. I had never felt so happy to see her. On the drive home she asked me to tell her what had happened. More importantly, she asked me how I was *feeling*.

'I feel embarrassed and sad, Mum,' I said, with my head down.

'Why do you feel like that, darling?' she asked warmly.

'No one's going to want to be my friend. Everyone's going to think I'm yuck,' I said, feeling at an all-time low.

In that moment, Mum was able to 'reality check' my emotional response. 'That's actually not true at all, darling. You're a lovely boy,' she assured me. 'The fact you had an accident doesn't stop you being a lovely boy. If you went back into the classroom now, people might think it was yucky, but no one will think that about you on Monday.'

As a parent and protector, Mum instinctively took control of my story and, by doing so, led me to a lighter place. Had she not asked me to tell her what I was feeling and thinking, a dark inner dialogue would have festered into a story of shame. I would have *believed* I was disgusting and that no one would want to be friends with me: a classic case of being ashamed about the person, not the act.

By the time Dad got home I felt a lot better than I had while hunched in a ball on the floor of the boys' toilets.

As Mum and I walked him through what had happened, Dad's sympathetic expression betrayed the beginnings of a smile. The more of the story he heard, the more I could see he was trying not to laugh. Far from being hurt or put out, I could see in the sparkle of his eyes that the episode wasn't the end of the world. By the time I'd finished the story, and had had a big cuddle with Dad, I could tell he was somewhat enthralled by it. By inviting him inside my little show-and-tell disaster zone and showing him around, it felt like we were in it together. In other words, sharing led to empathy, and remember, 'Shame cannot survive empathy.'

My parents – Mum in particular – were great at helping me manage my emotions. Unfortunately, our parents can't always be there to step in and diffuse every shame bomb (which have a habit of detonating later in life). Because it is a universal emotion, there is no avoiding shame.

With Anita's help I have come to realise every pang of shame I experience in my adult life can be traced back to a past event. What all these events have in common is that I *hadn't* been able to share them with Mum and Dad, or anyone else, at the time. Without empathy, these shame stories percolated in my psyche and went on to exert a negative and damaging influence on me.

To demonstrate, I'll revisit two of the shame stories I mentioned in the first chapter.

I'm not good-looking enough

When I was nine I joined my first sporting team – the mighty Balwyn Blazers Basketball Club. The joy and excitement I felt as Dad dropped me at the stadium for my first-ever training session was unparalleled at that point in my life. I bounced my brand-new basketball as I confidently approached a group of boys who were to be my new teammates and, even better, my new friends.

As I joined the throng of Under-10s, however, one of the boys took one look at me and started chuckling. He then pointed at my head and, in fits of laughter, said, 'Oh my God! Bugs Bunny is playing for us! You're not in our team, are you?'

This set some of the others off.

'Look at his teeth! They're just like Bugs Bunny's!'

'Oh my God, and he's got *huge* eyes!'

I smiled and pretended I thought it was funny. I then tried to join in, but every time I spoke someone would cut me off with, 'Err, what's up, Doc?'

To be fair to those kids, when I look back at photos of myself it's actually quite hard to disagree with their assessment. But at nine it was a crushing blow to my self-esteem. That night I cried in my room, alone. And so began a shame story: 'I'm not good-looking enough.'

For decades after, I felt self-conscious, particularly around girls – even in my mid-thirties. I'll never forget sitting across a table from my now wife Penny on our first date and thinking, Be funny, because she's *way* too good-looking for you. Nowadays as I watch our children play, I wonder how different my opinion of myself would have been had I gone home from basketball that night and shared that story with Mum and Dad, not sat in my room in tears.

I'm not smart enough

When I was in Year 9 at Carey Grammar I was selected in the First XI cricket team, which mainly comprised Year 12 boys. Coincidentally, my maths teacher also coached the First XI. We saw a lot of each other on Fridays since I started the day with maths and in the afternoon I traded a biro for a ball and boarded a bus with the big boys to go and play cricket. One Friday morning my maths class received some test results. My teacher hadn't marked my test yet. 'I'll give you yours at cricket this afternoon,' he said.

Later that day as the cricket team geared up for battle, my teacher handed me my test results – in front of some of the others. 'Thirty-eight per cent,' he said. 'Lowest mark in the class, Hugh.'

And just like that, a belief that I wasn't smart enough was born. The words 'lowest mark in the class' echoed in my head for the rest of the day. In time they morphed into the vicious three-word slogan, 'I am dumb.'

I'd love to go back in time and give 15-year-old Hugh a little pep talk in the cricket changing room. 'You're not dumb, mate. Maybe maths isn't your strong point. In fact, you are *terrible* at maths. But that doesn't make you dumb. You love English, you love writing, and you're good at history. But you will *never* need to use quadratic equations, I promise.'

Unfortunately, I lost my confidence in all subjects that day instead.

Such is the power of shame.

I'm well aware these shame stories didn't hold me back in life. In fact, by the time I reached Year 12, I had managed to reframe my 'not smart enough' shame story. I was lucky, though. Being good at sport gave me a confidence that spilt over into other areas. I'm also aware that on the 'shame spectrum' my stories are on the lower end. Many other people aren't so lucky – especially those shamed by those who are meant to love them and care for them.

In his groundbreaking book, *Healing the Shame That*

Binds You, American businessman and author John Bradshaw writes, 'Toxically shamed people tend to become more and more stagnant as life goes on. They live in a guarded, secretive and defensive way. They try to be more than human (perfect and controlling) or less than human (losing interest in life or stagnated in some addictive behavior.)'

I'm sharing my show-and-tell debacle and maths test humiliation stories to demonstrate how different the outcomes can be if we air our shame instead of hiding it. And if you're wondering what happened when I returned to school the Monday after I wet my pants, it went really well! I've faced some very high stakes situations in my time but nothing, *nothing* compares to walking back into that classroom. Quite early in the day I overheard one of my classmates beginning to tell another boy – who'd been absent from the fateful show-and-tell – about the high drama he had missed.

Remembering my lovely interaction with Dad, I decided to take control of the story, so I stepped in and gave the boy my own take on pissing my pants in front of the class. The kid laughed so hard I thought *he* was in danger of going down the same path. As the three of us cackled together, I realised I had found a way to feel good about something bad.

I shared it and let it go.

■

Show-and-tell wasn't the last time I screwed up in front of a crowd. I've given more than five thousand talks since 2010 and made a fool of myself more times than I care to remember. One occasion, however, stands out.

In 2019, I was due to give a talk at the Melbourne Convention Centre. At the time I was doing a huge amount of running and had aggravated a condition in my left knee called patellar tendinopathy. It's an extremely painful injury and if I stood for more than forty-five minutes it would become excruciating. I could only manage it if I took anti-inflammatory drugs.

Since I had to be on a plane to Sydney early the next morning, I'd got a prescription for Temazepam, a sleeping tablet. The plan was to take one immediately after finishing the Convention Centre talk. Speaking to large audiences gives me such a buzz it can be ages before I'm able to wind down. Sometimes I've been unable to get to sleep until 6 am.

Sitting in the green room just before I was due to walk onstage, I reached for my anti-inflammatories and washed one down with a swig of water. When I tossed the pills back into my bag I saw 'Temazepam' printed in black letters on the bottom of the blister pack. 'Holy shit!' I yelped, and rushed over to the sink. I jammed my fingers down my throat in an attempt to throw up, but I've never been able to pull that off. I don't seem to have a gag reflex. Still, I had to try. I was bent over the sink with my hand shoved wrist deep into my mouth when a lovely usher walked in and announced it was time for me to go on.

When he saw me trying to vomit he was very kind. 'You must be pretty nervous,' he said reassuringly. 'I've heard a lot of people get sick before they have to perform. Don't worry, I'm sure you'll be great as soon as you get onstage.'

How I wished it was nerves instead of Temazepam. Oh my God, I thought, as my iron stomach flat out refused to give the pill up. I am about to fall asleep in front of 2600 people who have come to hear me talk about resilience.

As I walked onto the stage I had just one thought: How long until I face-plant and start drooling on the floor? I can't honestly claim that in that moment I recalled the lessons learnt from owning the show-and-tell pants-wetting, but I have no doubt my subconscious went to work. I knew the only way I was going to survive the imminent disaster was if I owned it and shared it.

'Okay, tonight I'd like to begin with a bit of a warning, I suppose you'd have to call it,' I said to the audience. 'This is not a joke or a part of the talk, but I have just accidentally swallowed a sleeping tablet instead of the anti-inflammatory I meant to take.'

The audience burst out laughing, obviously in the belief I was kidding. 'No, no,' I said, 'I can't stress enough: this is not a part of my talk. I have actually screwed up. I took a tablet by mistake about ten minutes ago. I'm just letting you know because I don't know what's going to happen here.'

The pitch of the laughter changed from warmly conspiratorial to some scattered, nervous giggles.

With the confession/warning out of the way I launched into my speech. After about forty-five minutes I felt the chemicals going to work. A numbness rolled over me; I felt limp and relaxed, as if the power to my muscles had been cut and my joints had been filled with warm oil. My mouth, however, was as dry as the Sahara and I could barely speak.

Oh no! Here it comes, I thought.

Knowing there were some of our staff scattered around the auditorium I sent out a distress call. 'Um, if any Resilience Project staff are available I'd kill for a Coke right now,' I said. I wondered if it was just me who thought my voice sounded thick and slow. I also wondered what sort of presenter pauses a talk in order to ask someone to bring them a Coke.

As always, our CEO Ben was there to save me. He'd sprinted to a vending machine, wrestled a Pepsi out of it in world record time and handed it to an audience member who approached the stage to give it to me. Through the gathering numbness I heard myself say, 'What the fuck is this? I asked for a Coke!'

Apparently it was funny because people laughed. They laughed again when I stood in the middle of the stage and skolled the drink as if I was the Solo Man. The little hit of sugar and caffeine proved useless against the tide of Temazepam flooding my bloodstream. But it *did* give me a bad case of gas. I spent the next three minutes burping, not unlike Barney from *The Simpsons*.

Unbelievably, I managed to stay upright and make it through to the end. I put it down to one part adrenaline and nine parts audience support. It may not have been my sharpest ever presentation but it was definitely the most intimate.

In making myself vulnerable at the outset – by owning my massive screw-up – the other people in the room had empathy for me. Far from the night being a disaster, it ended up being the most bonding experience I've ever had with a group of strangers. The audience was connected and engaged in the event because they'd been invited to climb into the trenches with me. Like me, they found themselves wondering if I was going to collapse at any minute and, like me, they willed me to go on.

Professional mentor and leadership coach Ben Crowe has built a career on helping elite athletes such as Andre Agassi, Ash Barty and Stephanie Gilmore address their shame. One of Ben's key messages is to 'own your story'. Going over your past with a fine-tooth comb, however, can be easier said than done. As Ben points out, 'We are shit scared what we might find.'

EXERCISE
Dear Me . . .

Not everyone is in a position to work with a Ben Crowe, or a qualified counsellor or therapist, but this shouldn't stop us from exploring our shame stories. A useful first step is taking the time to write a letter to your younger self. A kind letter. It might be to the nine-year-old you or the fifteen-year-old version, but it needs to address the genesis of your shame. In my case, I wrote to Year 9 Hugh – the zinc-smeared, whites-wearing kid who believed he was an academic dunce. What would a younger, ashamed version of you want to hear from the adult you've become?

Map your life

To help you compose the letter, draw up a timeline of events that have helped shape the person you are today. List ten difficult things you have been through and ask yourself, 'Have any of them led to shameful thoughts?'

Then, on a separate piece of paper, make a list of all the strengths you now have as a result of those difficult episodes in your life.

It's also helpful to simply look around you at others who own their story, and recognise the strength and purpose it gives them. In my life that person is Georgia – no one has owned their story better than my sister. When I once said to her, 'I'm still angry at that fuck-up of a human who assaulted you,' she replied, 'I'm not. I've made peace with it. In fact, it's led me down the most amazing path. Look at all I'm now doing to help young people who are also affected by trauma. I wouldn't be doing any of this. And by the way, neither would you.'

I haven't quite attained Georgia's level of self-determination but I'm working on it.

46

EXPECTATION

CHAPTER 3
THE BEAUTIFUL
BREAKDOWN

Who'd have ever thought it would come to this?

A global pandemic. Airlines grounded. Borders closed. Face masks wherever we go. Virtual meetings. Outbreaks. Lockdowns. Isolation. Variants.

Yet as I write this we are two years in to the COVID-19 pandemic and what was once beyond comprehension is now depressingly familiar – the 'new normal' as some like to say. It's tempting to look back on life pre-COVID as carefree halcyon days when everything was easy, relaxed, uncom-plicated and overflowing with joy and peace. But human existence – the white-knuckle roller-coaster ride that careens precariously between our birth and inevitable death – is by nature a struggle. It might *seem* like a virus has derailed life as we know it but the truth is we've been running off the rails for a very long time.

Although COVID-19 has had a devastating impact on our way of life, we shouldn't forget how messed up we already were. Data published by the World Health Organization in 2017 placed Australia among the worst in the world when it comes to depression. Alongside Estonia and the US, the Lucky Country (with 5.9 per cent of the population affected) came in second only to the Ukraine (6.3 per cent).[1]

The statistics are even worse for our young people. A survey by Resilient Youth Australia found a staggering 40 per cent of secondary school students face mental health problems. Even more concerning is that 24 per cent of 9–12-year-olds also reported mental health issues.[2] That's one in four primary school kids!

There are countless reasons for poor mental health, ranging from conflict and trauma to serious illness and even genetics. In many cases we have no say in the matter, such as when we lose a loved one, experience a marriage breakdown or are subject to mental or physical abuse. Other causes of poor mental health, like the toxic shame we looked at in the previous chapters, evolve over time inside our heads without input from anyone else. One such factor that caused me unexpected stress and worry was the scourge of unreasonable expectations.

Expectation has been described as 'premeditated resentment'. We feel let down when the expectations we have of others aren't met. When we don't live up to the expectations we place on ourselves, we can end up feeling like a failure, ashamed and unworthy of love. It's one thing to feel like we have let someone else down but when we disappoint ourselves, the critical self-talk can run on a loop.

So often, the expectations we place on ourselves are unfair and unreasonable. We set ourselves these lofty standards, often subconsciously, and end up drowning in negative emotions when we don't live up to them. We never really question them, either. We never sit down and analyse where they came from. If you actually articulate your expectations, you will notice that they often start with the words 'I have to'. For example:

- I have to exercise every day.
- I have to make sure the house is clean all the time.

- I have to make everyone feel happy when they are in my company.
- I have to be entertaining when I'm with these people.

We never ever question why we *have to* do these things.

'*Why* do I have to exercise every single day?' The answer is to get fit, and that's great, but we can miss a day here or there and still achieve a good outcome. We don't need to be so hard on ourselves for not being perfect.

When the house is spotless I feel calm. Again, that's a great way to feel, but if you're in lockdown, with kids, that expectation is unrealistic. We need to start cutting ourselves some slack in order to avoid the negative emotions that come with unrealistic expectations. I know this all too well.

The expectation I placed on myself as a teenager was a doozy. Not only was I adamant that I had to be okay, it was up to me to make *everyone* else okay, too. As I tried to live up to this as an adult, I spent ten years travelling the country talking in schools, workplaces, sporting clubs, boardrooms and community halls, desperately trying to help people fly against the terrible headwinds of Australia's growing mental health crisis.

In hindsight, the expectation I placed on myself worked well, a lot of the time. Luckily, I have genuinely felt very okay for most of my life. I have never experienced mental ill health and would describe myself as a joyful person. But like anyone, I have my ups and downs, and when I feel down, this expectation to always be okay has proved disastrous. Towards the end of 2019 – before COVID-19 had even arrived on the scene – I felt myself heading into a steep dive.

In the final week of the working year I was booked to give multiple talks across two states. First up, I had the Essendon Football Club on the Monday morning. Then I was due to race across town to address a corporate audience at one of the big four banks in the afternoon. The following day I was scheduled to fly to Queensland to work with the Gold Coast Suns Football Club before driving from Coolangatta to the Sunshine Coast for a three-day session with the Port Adelaide Football Cub. It was an intense schedule to close out the year.

The moment I awoke on the Monday morning, though, I felt like a ghost – more hollow and drained of life than I ever had felt before. My emotional well was dry; there was nothing more to give. I couldn't even pretend to be okay so I just lay still. Although I hadn't said a word, my intuitive wife Penny, then pregnant with our daughter Elsie, did her best to roll over. She smiled at me. 'Just one more week to go,' she said.

I wasn't the only one in need of a break. My constant travel and relentless workload meant Penny was left to run the house and care for our son Benji largely by herself. Her job grew more and more demanding as Benji bloomed from a toddler into a little boy. 'I'll take the dog for a walk and you can get Benji up,' she suggested and left the room in search of a dog leash.

'Okay,' I groaned.

A few minutes later Penny poked her head back into the bedroom. 'What are you doing?' she asked.

I hadn't got Benji up. I hadn't moved an inch. And now I was crying. *Really* crying.

'What's wrong?' Penny asked.

'I can't get out of bed,' I sobbed. 'I don't know why. I just can't.'

'What are you talking about?' Penny sounded confused and made a face that said, 'Should I be worried or are you just taking the piss?'

'I'm not sure what's going on,' I spluttered. 'I just can't do this. I can't do anything. I don't have it in me.'

Eventually I got myself together enough to phone our CEO Ben to get a read on how it would go down if I pulled the pin on the week's commitments.

Ben was sympathetic and said he'd make some calls, but

I knew I'd be letting everyone down. 'These people booked me a year ago. That's not going to be an easy phone call to make – and it doesn't look good on a company called The Resilience Project,' I pointed out.

'You're right,' Ben conceded.

I dragged myself out of bed and started putting one foot in front of the other. Two hours later I was standing in front of the entire playing group at the Essendon Football Club. Usually, as I'm being introduced to an audience before I speak, I tell myself to make this the best thing they have ever seen. Almost like a last-minute mantra before I get into it. It sounds ridiculously arrogant but it gets me into a good headspace before I do something that requires a lot of confidence. On this day the mantra I told myself was simpler: Just get through this.

I have very little recollection of what I said that morning or how it was received. I did, however, achieve the not so lofty goal of getting through it. When I got back to my car I was relieved to discover Ben had made some calls and managed to reschedule the talk with the bankers for the new year.

The next morning I was on a flight to the Gold Coast. As I arrived at the Suns' home ground I had serious doubts I'd be able to get through it. I gave it absolutely everything I could and headed to my hotel room feeling achingly homesick – a miserable sensation I hadn't experienced since school camp in Year 6. I desperately wanted to be with Penny and Benji in Melbourne.

The feeling of hopelessness carried through to Wednesday. I hired a car for the two-and-a-half-hour drive to Maroochydore where Port Adelaide was staging its pre-season camp. I genuinely love the people at the Port Adelaide Football Club. I'd done a lot of work with the club over the previous two seasons and normally I was excited to be around them. On this particular day, though, I felt like I was driving into a nightmare.

Two weeks earlier in Adelaide I'd told the players I'd be joining them for some sessions in Maroochydore, and outlined what I had planned. 'On the first night of camp I'm going to ask you to do something incredibly courageous,' I said.

It wasn't the kind of courage they were used to – the kind that could result in broken bones. No, I asked them to take an emotional risk by sharing their real story, from the heart. I invited them to do something that's scary for a lot of Australian men (and women) – I asked them to be vulnerable.

'We put on armour before we venture out into the world,' I explained. 'We want to protect ourselves from opinions, judgement and anything else that could potentially hurt us psychologically. So we armour up. The issue is, this armour prevents us from making genuine, authentic and life-changing connections. So, on night two of our camp,' I continued, after having gained approval from the club psychologist, 'I'm going to give you the opportunity to take the armour off and tell us your real story. It's not compulsory, by the way – forced vulnerability does not count – but if we get a few people to speak their truth, I promise you that it will connect us. That's what we're about here at Port. Authentic connection.'

It had sounded like a great idea two weeks before, but now it seemed like a recipe for disaster. With zero emotional energy left to draw on, how could I facilitate a session where I asked men – whose lives were all about being as tough as nails – to stand up and be vulnerable? If I was an emotional blank it would be a catastrophe.

The more I thought about this, the more I realised the session simply couldn't happen. As I made my way up the M1 I decided I'd just say my flight had been cancelled. Just as I'd made that decision a minibus full of the club's younger players drove by. I'd been spotted. There was no backing out now.

As I drew closer to my destination I turned on the radio in an attempt to distract myself. As soon as I did I was surprised to hear a song that had been a huge favourite of mine fifteen years before. My first year as a young primary schoolteacher in Melbourne had been stressful. To get myself into a good headspace before work, I'd often play the soundtrack to one of my favourite movies, *Garden State*. My favourite song on the album was 'Let Go' by the British band Frou Frou. And now it filled the car as I closed in ominously on Maroochydore. Due to copyright, I can't reproduce the exact words of the song's chorus, but in a nutshell, Frou Frou urge us to just let go and jump on in because there's 'beauty in the breakdown'.

I must have listened to those lyrics a thousand times before without a second's thought. On this day, however, they caused me to burst into tears (again). The song triggered potent memories of the times that I knew I hadn't been okay but chose to plough on, acting as if everything was totally fine – a hostage to my expectations. It also triggered memories of people I'd met along life's highway: people who'd shown me that, yes, there *is* beauty in the breakdown.

When vulnerability meets expectation

Vulnerability, that paradoxically powerful willingness to expose ourselves to emotional risk, can help solve so many of our woes. It can even free us from the pressure of our expectations. After all, that's why I asked the Port Adelaide players to share difficult stories from the heart. Thanks to Frou Frou, by the time I arrived in Maroochydore I'd decided I owed these boys my vulnerability, too.

I was a long way from feeling okay and I still wanted to go home but for the first time in a long time I decided I wasn't going to pretend. I always put a lot of effort into the first two minutes of a talk. You've only got a short amount of time to win over an audience and for them to decide if they're going to listen to you or not. The format for my first two minutes is always the same: be funny and self-deprecating. On this night, and maybe for the first time ever, I did away with the format.

'I'm totally and utterly exhausted,' I began, my heart pounding. 'I'm burnt out. I'm emotionally exhausted and as much as I love you boys, I just want to be at home with my wife Penny and my son Benji.'

The room suddenly felt very tense. An especially big player in the front row who'd been munching on a protein bar stopped mid-chew as if to emphasise the awkwardness. 'Um, it's been a long year,' I continued. 'Right now I am the most homesick I have ever felt. But this is a really important session for us. There's no way I was going to miss it and I'm looking forward to it. So I'm just going to hand over to you guys. Is anyone up for sharing their story?'

One of the younger players from the minibus, 19-year-old Zak Butters, got to his feet. 'I'll go first,' he said. Over the next fifteen minutes Zak told us a heartbreaking story that took place the previous season, his first year in the AFL. As tears streamed down the young man's face he revealed that his older sister had disappeared. The police had come to the family home and his sister was listed as a missing person. It turned out she had struggled with drug addiction. It was two weeks before she was finally found.

Hardly anyone at the club had known about it. But now, as Zak laid himself bare through his willingness to be vulnerable, you could feel the love and empathy of the group wrap around him. Zak's courage set the tone for the rest of the session and over the next few hours, fifteen more men stood up and shared difficult truths and heartbreaking episodes from their lives.

The night proved to be a potent tonic for my battered psyche. The superpower those men tapped into sparked something magical for us all. The bonds made were immediate, strong and undeniable. Once you open yourself up like that, there's no going back to the status quo – you are in it together for the long run. That's the power of authentic connection.

Having dreaded the occasion to the point of almost

bailing out, I found it hard to say goodbye when the Maroochydore trip was over. If I'm honest, part of me wanted to stay longer. I still missed my family desperately and I was anxious to get home, but the breakdown I felt I'd been on the verge of having for three days had turned out to be something else. It had turned out to be beautiful.

When I left the players on the Friday I marvelled at the power of vulnerability. Like a tractor beam, it had pulled me out of an emotional black hole. I had then watched it knit a group of people closer together than I think we ever thought was possible. In time, the seeds planted that night would show in their performance, too. Port Adelaide finished on top of the ladder in 2020, one of the best results in the club's history. To be very clear, I am not saying this was because of me or our session. They were an incredible bunch of players with an amazing coaching staff. In every single post-match interview, however, I heard the players say a version of, 'We've got a very special connection at this club.' They are the ones who took the emotional risks that night. They are the ones who deserve the credit.

I cued up Frou Frou on Spotify for the long drive back to Coolangatta and played 'Let Go' on repeat the whole way. En route to the camp it was the lyric 'let go' that gave me strength. On the way home from the camp, however, it was the lyric 'there's beauty in the breakdown' that really spoke to me. There was so much beauty in what had happened in just seven days. The reason our breakdowns are beautiful, I concluded, is that when we surrender and concede that we are at a low point we are then flooded with a sense of humility and curiosity. For me, the humility enabled me to forgive myself for not being okay all the time. And the curiosity gave me insight into where my deep-seated expectation had come from in the first place.

I wish I could say I had things figured out in 2019 and that after spending the summer holidays with my family I reset my expectations, but as you'll see in the next chapter, I was a slow learner.

CHAPTER 4

DEMONS

Like many businesses that operate in the mental health space, The Resilience Project experienced a surge in demand after COVID-19 took hold in Australia in early 2020. Although a flurry of lockdowns and travel restrictions in the following months put an end to our ability to connect with communities face to face, Zoom and our digital program allowed us to keep 'showing up'. Instead of talking in schools, town halls or the conference rooms of corporations, we 're-tooled' to host sessions online. I also kept up the radio interviews to try to help in any way I could.

A few weeks before my on-air 'I'm totally and utterly broken' moment, I was speaking on another FM radio station. Five minutes in to what I was told would be a fifteen-minute interview, the host cut in and said, 'Good on ya, champion, this is great stuff. Now let's check the traffic with Stevo in the chopper!' I didn't even get a chance to say thanks for having me before I was hit with the dial tone. Ah well, you win some you lose some, I thought to myself. Or, more aptly, as a mate once said to me, 'You win some, you lose most.'

Five minutes later my phone rang. It was a private number. I don't usually answer calls from numbers I don't recognise, but I find a private number hard to resist.

'Hello, Hugh speaking.'

'Hi Hugh, this is Steve,' the voice said.

'What, from the helicopter?' I responded, shocked.

'I beg your pardon?' said Steve, who clearly *wasn't* in a helicopter.

'Sorry, wrong Steve!' I said, trying not to laugh. 'How can I help you?'

'I just heard you on the radio. I work for a supermarket and was wondering if you could come and work with my team.'

'Oh, thank you, mate,' I replied. 'Maybe just send an

email to our website and Laura will get back to you.' I wasn't trying to give him the brush off, it's just that I'm hopeless at the administrative side of things and thankfully have a team who are far better equipped to take bookings and organise my calendar.

'Oh,' he said, sounding a little surprised. There was an awkward pause. 'It's just that I have quite a big team here . . .'

'Good on you, mate,' I said, channelling the radio host who'd just hurried me off the air. 'Well, send that email to our website and if COVID-19 permits, I'll hopefully be able to get out to your store and give a talk.'

'I'm not in a store,' Steve persisted. 'I'm at head office.'

'Right, sorry, well if you send that email to the website I'll hopefully be able to come to the head office. How many people do you have in your team there, Steve?'

'Ah, one hundred and twenty thousand,' he replied evenly.

'Pardon?' I squeaked.

'I'm the CEO, Hugh.'

'Oh, okay, good, lovely, that's great,' I fumbled in reply.

'At a time like this, I need to be doing everything I can to support the incredible people in my team. Can you and your company deliver a wellbeing program to one hundred and twenty thousand people?'

'Yes, of course we can,' came my way too hasty and presumptuous response.

'Excellent. Let's make this happen then,' said Steve, probably still wondering why I'd thought he was in a helicopter.

Over the next few weeks our team put together a program for all employees at the supermarket chain – a partnership I am very proud of. Part of the program involved online sessions where staff could join a psychologist and me for what we called 'peer learning'. We encouraged employees to be vulnerable and share issues they were struggling with. It was a simple idea: a safe (albeit virtual) place where people could open up.

Some of the Zoom sessions were extremely moving. In the middle of Melbourne's gruelling second lockdown a middle-aged man unmuted abruptly and said, 'I'm really battling, guys. This lockdown is really taking a toll emotionally. I feel broken. What do I do about it?'

'I'm battling too,' I admitted. 'So, I'm potentially not the person to tell you what to do right now but I will say this – you need to speak to a qualified therapist. It could be a counsellor, a social worker, a psychologist. If you don't feel like doing that, at the very least you need to speak to a friend.'

He umm-ed and ahh-ed a little so I went on a bit of an unsolicited rant. 'Mate, if you've got dental problems, you see a dentist. If you've got an injury, you see a physio. So why should it be different for issues you have emotionally and mentally? If you've got mental health issues, you need to see a mental health professional.'

'That's easy enough to say,' he replied. 'But I have no idea where to start, or how to find one. And how do I find one I like? I'd also be a bit uncomfortable about telling people I'm seeing a psychologist, to be honest with you. You obviously see one, so how did you find yours?'

'Actually, I don't see a psychologist,' I confessed. This was before I began seeing Anita.

'*Really?*' he said, sounding surprised.

'Yeah,' I replied. 'Actually, I've never seen one.'

'Are you serious? So how come you tell everyone else to see a psychologist when you don't do it yourself?'

'That's an excellent question,' I said. 'I think you're right to point that out . . . you know what? I'm going to find a psychologist. But I want you to promise me you will, too.'

It's interesting that of all the people I could have dropped my guard with I chose a group of total strangers, and not even in person – on a Zoom call! But at least I'd done it and, by saying the words out loud, my lockdown struggles suddenly became very real to me. As I started casting around for a psychologist that afternoon, I realised the guy from the conference call had raised more than one valid concern.

For example, just how *do* you find a psychologist who's right for you? Due to my line of work I know some wonderful psychologists. My first instinct was to ask them all for their best recommendation. As I pondered this, however, I couldn't help but remember the number of times people have collared me after a talk and said, 'You don't understand how hard it is to find a professional to speak to.' I decided I would look for a mental health professional the same way anyone else would in order to experience the process.

Over a few weeks I made random appointments with four different practitioners. I discovered the first one while sitting in traffic near home. I just looked out the window and saw the clinic. Oh, that's a nice logo, and what excellent branding, I mused. That will do me just fine.

I parked the car, walked in and made an appointment.

The first session got off to a disappointing start when the psychologist descended a set of stairs and greeted me by waving an EFTPOS machine. She didn't even say hello. 'Can you pay now?' she asked. 'I hate walking down the stairs after a session to do the payment.'

Why I didn't give her the radio host's 'Good on ya, champion' and walk out I will never know. The session was a disaster and I left feeling awful. None from one.

My second session was across town. I had chosen this

person somewhat randomly, after spending ages online scrolling through the profiles of different psychologists all over Melbourne. As I sat down the guy said, 'Just so you know, I'm going to drink coffee.' He had his own little espresso pod machine on a cabinet behind him. Now, I'm probably being a little bit petty here but . . . he didn't offer me one! Not that I was dying for a coffee but I worried that the person I was about to pour my heart out to had the social skills of a three-year-old. None from two.

For my third session, I quite literally chose the clinic closest to my home. A five-minute walk, in fact. The session was fine. She was a lovely person. But when you are divulging your life story to a stranger you deserve better than fine. None from three.

In frustration I relented and called my friend Maria, who is an excellent psychologist. 'Can I please see you?' I begged.

'No, you can't,' she replied flatly. 'Because then we would have to stop being friends and I don't want that. However, I'm going to put you in touch with an incredible woman. Her name is Anita.'

By that stage I'd just had my impromptu mini-meltdown on live radio, a declaration to the country that I was struggling mentally. I was really hoping that Anita would work out.

In the time it had taken me to get comfortable in her chair, I could already tell Anita was warm, empathetic and very professional. Too often in life, whenever I've felt awkward or uncomfortable, I've used humour as a kind of camouflage to hide my feelings. It's also a great way of getting people to like me on first meeting. As I sat in the chair, the impulse to be funny was too much to resist. So I reeled off some amusing anecdote from my morning. Anita smiled patiently as I got it over and done with. Then she offered a small, polite laugh. She'd seen it all before. Anita didn't mind that I felt awkward and she didn't care that I wanted her to like me. She wasn't there to be my friend – she was there to help. In that one restrained laugh, I knew she was 'the one'.

After setting out guidelines and objectives for the session Anita asked me where I'd like to start. As I sometimes do with difficult subjects, I backed into the topic obliquely by using an obscure reference and someone else's words to describe my feelings. 'I think my life right now can be summed up by the lyric of a song,' I told her. It was a tune by my favourite band, The National, and, funnily enough, it was called 'Demons'. In it the singer Matt Berninger laments that whenever he walks into a room, he is unable to 'light it up'.

'That describes me so well at the moment,' I told Anita. 'Ever since I can remember I have felt like my superpower was the ability to light up a room; to put smiles on everyone's faces. For some reason I have always felt it was my job to make everyone feel happy. I was very good at it.'

I explained this self-imposed expectation had taken root during my sister's battle with anorexia and out of my desire to lift the mood of our devastated family. Since those teenage days it had mushroomed into an obsession that permeated every aspect of my existence, from my family and work environment right down to my social life and even casual acquaintances. The second I felt that anyone was down, or even just not having a good time, I felt anxiety come over me. You have to do something, Hugh, I would tell myself. Make these people happy.

As Anita listened I was at pains to convey just how all-consuming this expectation was. I considered telling her a story that would leave her in no doubt but thought better of it as I was extremely embarrassed by it and thought it would make a terrible impression. For the purpose of this chapter, however, I'll share it with you.

At the age of 22 I went on my first-ever end-of-season football trip, to Adelaide. If you haven't been on one all you need to know is that these things were originally designed for elite footballers who spend ten months not drinking, not going to bars, pubs or nightclubs, and following a very strict diet. The idea is that in the space of a few days they get to do all the things they haven't been able to do for ten months, as far from home as possible so that they are less likely to be recognised.

How this concept extended to local clubs around the country I'll never understand. The experience of playing local footy involves a lot of drinking, going out every Saturday night, eating whatever the hell you want and being recognised by absolutely no one. Regardless, end-of-season trips are a rite of passage for local clubs across the country.

Our first night out in Adelaide was an eye-opener. The excitement levels were so high that most people didn't go to bed. My two hours of sleep was described by one of the senior players as 'very responsible behaviour'.

At 10 am the next day all forty of us assembled in the hotel bar. Not surprisingly, the mood was down. The group was flat. I was acutely uncomfortable with the lack of energy and happiness in the room. I was almost anxious. People are unhappy, do something, my inner voice urged.

Without really having a plan I pulled one of the guys aside and told him to get everyone out the front of the hotel in five minutes' time. 'I'm just going to disappear for a bit but if you make sure they're all out the front I'll have something for them,' I said.

Still with no idea what I was going to do I jogged down the street, away from the pub, and conceived the vague idea of making a grand re-entrance in front of everyone. I was two city blocks away when I decided the only way to truly lift spirits and bring joy would be to reappear *in the nude*.

Standing in the Adelaide CBD with my friends' happiness hanging in the balance, I took all of my clothes off, save for my socks and shoes. (I can't believe I'm admitting to this on the record – sorry, Mum and Dad. Actually, this may not surprise them, I should probably apologise to my in-laws, Rob and Anne, instead.) My hastily constructed 'plan' was to jog past the pub naked as if it were a perfectly normal thing to do – just a man out for a bit of exercise. Surely *that* would put smiles on faces!

As the guys assembled on the verandah outside the hotel I set off at a nice, steady jogging pace doing my best Steve Moneghetti impersonation. I hadn't run fifty metres before I was overtaken by a male cyclist in full Lycra and those wrap-around sunglasses.

'You're a fucking idiot!' he yelled as he swept past me.

You are correct, I thought to myself. However, his drive-by sledge had the same effect on me as a starter's pistol.

I was off! I accelerated into a full sprint, knees high, arms swinging as I set off in pursuit of the middle-aged man in Lycra.

As I drew close to the pub I started to close the gap on him. When my mates saw me running along the middle of the road completely nude a great roar went up. The cyclist gave the boys a wave of acknowledgement, thinking they were cheering for him, which only made them cheer louder. At the very moment we reached the pub the cyclist turned around and caught sight of me, only five metres or so behind him in full, naked flight.

'What the fuck!?' he yelled out in shock.

He then got out of the saddle, put his head down and started peddling like a mad man. I too went up a gear. Knees even higher now, driving my arms to reach maximum speed. The two of us flew past the hotel side by side. Never in my life had I heard laughter like it.

Soon the laughter faded. With the 'job done' I slowed as the cyclist sped away, leaving me alone, naked and quite puffed.

I caught a glimpse of myself in a shop window. Christ, what *am* I doing? I thought. I was well past the pub and pretty much stranded. My clothes were in a pile on the footpath about three city blocks away. I couldn't retrace my steps past the pub because it would ruin the moment that I had just put myself on the line to create, so I disappeared around the next corner and looped back around the city blocks to my starting point.

Now, I accept it's unlikely that you have ever been naked in the middle of a major city – especially at 10 o'clock in the morning – but let me assure you that once the adrenaline has worn off and you are all alone, there is a fair amount of shame involved. There was a technical–legal side to my antics, too: under the South Australian Crimes Act, 'indecent behaviour' is punishable by three months in prison, and I had been most indecent.

I'd had such tunnel vision about improving the mood for my friends that none of this had entered my mind when I set off. It sure as hell was front and centre during the walk of shame back to my clothes. I kept my eyes focused on the ground as I darted along the streets and scurried past shop-fronts, suddenly and rightfully fearful of offending anyone.

Ten minutes later I was fully clothed and back in the pub, acting as if I'd just stepped out to make a phone call. The joint was absolutely humming as I innocently played dumb. 'Have I missed something? What happened?'

When I look back at that day now, almost twenty years later, I cringe with embarrassment. But it underscores the extreme pressure I felt to 'light up a room'. It wasn't a one-off, either. Hell, I ended up building a career out of it (performing that is, not doing nude runs). The expectations I have placed on myself have been my undoing on so many occasions. For so long, I have honestly felt as though other people's emotions are my responsibility.

'And now I can't do it anymore,' I lamented to Anita. 'I couldn't light up a room with a flamethrower at the moment. It's like the thing that made me *me* has gone and I'm feeling very, very lost.'

'How are you able to do your job?' she asked.

'Oh, professionally, it's not a problem. My talks are second nature to me now,' I explained. 'It's social situations. Among groups of people, whom I love and know well, I just can't do it anymore.'

I pushed a little for answers. 'I don't know if I've lost the ability altogether,' I said out loud. 'Or if it's just the fact that I am totally and utterly exhausted.'

We didn't get to the answer straight away. It surfaced a couple of months later, once we'd revealed the shame I felt about my sister. Expecting us to continue discussing the situation with Georgia, I was surprised when Anita quoted the song lyric I'd mentioned in our first-ever session back to me. She then asked me a very pointed question.

'Who is expecting you to light up the room, Hugh?'

'Everyone,' I replied quickly. 'Mum and Dad, my brother, my friends, my colleagues. *Everyone.*'

'*Everyone?*' she asked. 'Your mum and dad expect you to light up the room whenever they see you?'

That question hit me like a punch in the face. I instantly recalled all the times I'd left Mum and Dad's house feeling disappointed in myself because I hadn't been hilariously entertaining.

'Do your parents really have that expectation of their son?'

'Of course they don't,' I said, shaking my head and wondering how I'd ever come to that conclusion.

'And your friends,' Anita gently pushed. 'Do they expect that of you?'

'I'm sure they're happy whenever I do, but it's certainly not an expectation they have.'

To think I could have saved myself from running nude through the streets of Adelaide.

Later that week, as I reflected on my notes from that session, it dawned on me that we all place expectations on ourselves. Some of them are necessary in order to function as part of a community. But so many of them are not wedded to reality. We create these expectations based on what we think others expect from us. Or even worse, we allow others' expectations of us to have damaging influences on our lives.

Around the time of this breakthrough with Anita, I interviewed drive-time radio host Will McMahon from 'Will & Woody' for an episode of a podcast I co-host called *The Imperfects*. I was intrigued as he spoke about the expectations he felt saddled with courtesy of his private school education. 'Those expectations were the source of my, and so many of my friends', undoing,' he said. 'The expectation to excel academically, then go to university and then get a high-paying corporate job.'

At age 23 Will found himself on a very different path. When he realised it didn't merge with the expectations from his school days he spiralled into an awful depressive episode. It wasn't until he divorced himself from those expectations that he was able to move forward.

When I first sat down with Anita, I prefaced the session by saying I didn't have a mental illness per se. 'So I'll probably only need to see you once a month or maybe even less than that,' I said. 'I just want to check in now and then and talk about this stuff.'

In the space of two months, however, Anita had helped me to identify and free myself of shame and to understand that I was trying to live up to expectations that didn't exist. I was trapped by expectations that I had manufactured in my own head.

I very quickly scrapped the 'once a month' plan and arranged to see her once every two weeks for the remainder of 2020.

I don't know whether it's a normal thing to do but I would record each session on my phone and take copious amounts of notes. Then, a few days later, I'd listen back to the recording and make even more notes. It was as if I was studying Anita's study of me, and I was blown away by the stuff I learnt about myself.

About a week after my discovery on expectations I wrote myself three questions:

- What do my family expect of me?
- What do my colleagues expect from me?
- What do my friends expect from me?

After I answered these questions, I took time to consider the answers I'd given to each one. Are they true? Are they fair, to me and to them? If I concluded the answers weren't true or fair I made a pact with myself to break up with that expectation immediately. It was one of the most liberating things I have ever done. Nowadays it is such a beautiful thing when I visit my folks to simply show up as me, no matter what shape the day finds me in.

CONTROL

CHAPTER 5
A PAIN IN THE BUM

Back in 2005, I felt like my life was starting to take shape. I was 24 years old and only a few weeks into my first-ever teaching job. Although it was pretty stressful, having an income for the first time allowed me to rent a decent apartment in the inner Melbourne suburb of Richmond with my then girlfriend, Anjali, who was also starting out on her teaching career.

One morning, as sunlight filled our bedroom, I lay in bed happily, in the comfortable space between slumber and consciousness, clutching at the last wisps of sleep. I was starting to think about the day ahead when, with absolutely no warning, I found myself in the grip of a blinding pain. The appalling sensation was as excruciating as it was confronting. It felt like someone had shoved a cricket stump up my backside.

I let out an animal scream that made Anjali jolt awake and flail about in fear and confusion as if she, too, were under invisible attack.

'What's wrong?' she cried as I writhed beside her, still yelping in agony. 'Hugh! Talk to me! What's wrong?'

'*I . . . don't . . . know-w-w-w-w!*' I wailed as I grasped pathetically at my bum with both hands. Tears streamed down my face.

'Hugh?' Anjali said again, sounding panicked.

The pain was so intense I felt as if I might actually pass out. I screamed and sobbed, convinced I was undergoing a dramatic, life-changing event. 'I don't know what's going on,' I finally whimpered, 'but I have never felt . . .' Before I could finish the sentence the pain vanished as swiftly, completely and as weirdly as it had arrived.

'What the hell was all that about?' Anjali asked, looking horrified.

'I just . . . I dunno!' I panted. 'It was like someone grabbed a cricket stump and, yeah . . .'

I was just grateful it was over. And, now that it was, I became very self-conscious about the surprise early morning bum-attack. Embarrassment flushed my cheeks. Right, I thought. I'll just pretend *that* never happened.

'You need to go and get that checked out,' Anjali said evenly.

'Nah, I'll be fine,' I replied, eager to move onto another subject. One that didn't involve my anus. 'It was just one of those weird random things.' I swung my legs off the bed and stood up as if the past few minutes had never happened. 'Do you want a coffee?' I said.

The sudden macho insouciance didn't wash for one moment with the woman who had just been torn from a deep sleep by my guttural screams. 'I'm sorry,' she said, 'but that was *not* normal. You need to get it checked out by a doctor.'

'Pfff. Nah – seriously! I'm fine!' I said, taking control and starting to get ready for work. 'So, do you want a coffee?'

Boys don't cry, remember?

Over the next few days I threw myself into teaching my class of 10-year-olds at Melbourne's Fintona Girls' School, and all but forgot about the terrible dawn stumping.

A couple of weeks later I stood at the whiteboard with my back to the class and wrote out a maths lesson. Mathematics was never my strong suit, as you now know, and teaching it, even to 10-year-olds, caused me an enormous amount of stress. To prepare for the lesson, I had gone over the topic the night before, but now, as I scribbled it onto the board, it happened again. This time it was worse. The pain was so intense, I dropped to my knees, as if felled by a sniper. Bloody hell, the cricket stump is back! Not now, please not now! I pleaded to the gods.

The air filled with a weird, high-pitched noise. It took a moment for me to realise that the screaming was in fact coming from me, not the girls. Oh no, I thought. I twisted around to look at the class, unable to resist the compulsion to grab my bum. I needn't have worried about my students – far from being traumatised, they were in fits of laughter, some of them on the floor.

This time the pain didn't magically disappear. It felt endless. This boy most definitely did cry. There was a storeroom not far from where I'd collapsed and somehow I managed to half-roll, half-fall through the doorway. Once inside the tiny room I clutched again at my pain-besieged rear end.

After several minutes of torment and stifled sobbing, the crisis abruptly ended, once again without a hint there had ever been anything wrong.

'What happened, sir? Are you all right? Why are you crying?' A chorus of questions greeted me as I casually emerged from the storeroom as if I'd just popped in there to grab a new whiteboard marker.

'Me?' I said, looking confused by all the attention. 'I'm fine, why?'

'But you fell over and screamed!' one girl pointed out.

These kids weren't stupid. I had to come up with something to explain away the last few minutes but there was no way I was going to tell them the truth.

'It's totally fine,' I assured them. *What's a manly explanation?* Then I landed on it. 'I went for a massive run this morning, it was just a small cramp in my calf muscle, I think. All good.' I gave them two thumbs up and did my best to smile.

While the immediate physical crisis had passed, there was a fresh catastrophe unfolding in my mind. Oh my God! I've got prostate cancer!

The following afternoon I sat in a local medical centre across from a very attractive female doctor. I wished I'd drawn one of the older male practitioners instead but, since this was probably prostate cancer, I had to get over my embarrassment and tell this woman exactly what had happened.

'It all started a few weeks ago,' I began. 'Honestly, it was like someone had taken a cricket stump and rammed it as hard as they could up my . . .'

I didn't even need to finish my sentence before a small smile crept across her face. 'You don't have to explain,' she cut in. 'I know what this is.'

The doctor told me I had something called 'proctalgia fugax', a fairly common problem among uni students studying for high-pressure degrees such as medicine or law.

'Quite clearly it also affects at least one young primary schoolteacher!' she added. 'Proctalgia fugax is a condition where every muscle in your anus goes into spasm at once. It's a response to stress and it's your body's way of trying to stop it.'

'You've gotta be kidding me,' I said.

'I am not kidding you,' she deadpanned.

'So, when is it most likely to happen?'

'It's unpredictable.'

'Well, it can't happen in public!' I almost shouted.

'Sounds like it already has. If it happens again you'll just have to pretend you've got a cramp.'

I'd already tried that excuse with the girls at school.

'But you've never seen anyone carry on like this from a cramp,' I said. 'It's like . . . it's agony right up my bum!'

'Yes, yes, I know,' she said. 'It's every single muscle in your anus spasming and locking at once.'

I leant back, dragged my fingers through my hair and sighed. 'Oh, good God.'

As I left the medical centre I had just one thought on a loop: *Nobody* can know about this.

At the tender age of 24, I found myself saddled with a phantom condition that I had absolutely no control over. Proctalgia fugax wasn't only extremely embarrassing, I was also terrified people would associate it with weakness. The last thing I wanted was people thinking I wasn't okay: that I wasn't coping with my first year of teaching. That was *not* the image I'd been working hard to project.

The image I'd dreamt up for myself was of a young, laid-back, knockabout bloke. My hair was already receding and I'd grown it long and brushed it forward so no one could tell. The only threat to this scenario was a sudden gust of wind. To that end, I wore hats. A lot.

I had never surfed in my life back then, but I'd attempted to affect a beachy, sun-bleached vibe by using peroxide on my hair, too. I don't know why I was at pains to come across as easy-going and unflappable. The diagnosis that I was in fact so stressed that my arsehole would go into spasm wasn't a great fit.

Before I left the medical centre, the doctor had suggested I see a psychologist to help me deal with the underlying issues. 'It'd be worth talking with someone who's qualified to help you understand what's going on in your head,' she said.

My internal voice scoffed, Yeah-nah, that's not going to happen. But my outer voice politely said I'd consider it. By the time I got back to my car I was adamant that no one – not a shrink, not my family, not anyone on the face of the earth – would ever know about it.

I sat hunched over the steering wheel as worst-case scenarios flashed through my mind. What if it happened while I was driving? What if it happened in a supermarket? Or at the pub? Holy shit – what if it happened during school assembly? How would it look if I dropped to my knees in front of five hundred girls, crying and holding my bum cheeks? I would never recover. That's something you do not come back from.

The mental screening of these horror movies was interrupted by the electronic chirp of an incoming call. I looked at my phone and saw it was one of my best mates, Teddy. I love Teddy, but he was the *last* person I was going to talk to about my 'condition'.

Teddy and I had once gone away with a group of old school friends and their partners to a holiday house on the Mornington Peninsula. As we were the last to arrive, Teddy and I ended up sharing a room with a bunk bed. Always keen to avoid harm – physical or reputational – I had never told any of my friends that I suffered from night terrors. Even now I can't sleep in a room when it's pitch black because without fail I'll wake up screaming in the middle of the night.

That night as we climbed into our bunks and Teddy turned off the light, I knew exactly what was going to happen.

'Oh mate, that's quite dark,' I said. 'I might struggle to sleep.'

'You'll be fine,' said Teddy.

'Okay,' I said. 'But if I wake up in the night and I'm a bit confused, could you just remind me we're on the Mornington Peninsula on holiday and everything's gonna be fine?'

'Yeah, no worries,' he grunted and instantly fell asleep.

Sure enough, a few hours later, I sat bolt upright like a vampire in a coffin, shrieking at the top of my lungs. Terrified and with no idea where I was, I flung myself around in the darkness, banging into the walls in search of a doorway. Not surprisingly, Teddy woke up. But instead of playing his role and reassuring me that we were on holiday on the Mornington and that everything was okay, he employed a slightly different approach. At the top of his lungs he shouted, '*Ah, shut up, you maniac!*'

Kudos to Teddy, I snapped out of my night terror and went back to sleep. The next morning, however, I woke up cringing inwardly with embarrassment. When we all gathered for breakfast Teddy wasted no time in recounting the events of the previous night to our mates and their partners. 'Hey everybody, get a load of this!'

Now, as I sat in my car outside the medical centre, I decided to answer the call from Teddy. When I heard his familiar voice at the other end I was overcome by the need to tell him – to tell *someone* – what I'd suddenly found myself dealing with. I had only known for twenty minutes that proctalgia fugax was even a thing, but already I was finding it too much to keep to myself. I let Teddy in on my terrible secret, starting with a description of the cricket stump.

'Jesus,' he said when I'd finished. 'That sounds horrendous. What did you say it was called again?'

'Proctalgia fugax,' I replied. 'But I'm only telling you so I can get it off my chest. Don't tell anyone. I don't want anyone to know about it.'

'Yeah, mate, what a pain in the arse that is,' he said, giggling.

We made a loose plan to catch up for a beer down the track and said our goodbyes.

Back then there were no WhatsApp groups, no DMs or even smartphones. Information was shared by slightly slower means. When I got home that night I switched on my laptop and opened up my email. The inbox was full of messages under the subject heading, 'Hugh's bottom!'

Teddy had sent a group email to around ten of our close mates from our high school days:

Boys, I just spoke to Hugh and he's been diagnosed with a condition called Proctalgia Hugh-jax or something like that. It literally means he gets so stressed out that his bum hurts!

As I read the email my hands started shaking. My social life was dying before my very eyes. Oh no! I thought. They're all going to tell their girlfriends and everyone's going to know!

It was on. Bum gag after bum gag came flooding in via email. 'Thanks for the up(the)date,' read one of my favourites.

I felt exposed, ashamed and extremely embarrassed.

I felt vulnerable.

I had lost control of the situation.

Then a funny thing happened. Over the next couple of hours, most of the ten guys phoned me to see if I was okay. That single email – the sharing of my vulnerability that I had dreaded – unleashed a torrent of love and genuine concern for my wellbeing. Admittedly some of it was couched in deeply blokey terms ('Mate, is your bum all right? Tell me what's goin' on!') but all of them concluded their calls by saying they hoped I was okay and that they were there for me.

It was a stunning turnaround. That afternoon I'd felt frightened, alone, embarrassed and ashamed. That night I went to bed feeling loved, encouraged, relieved and grateful that so many people knew about my peculiar health complaint.

Thinking back on it I realised I'd also experienced the same kind of empathy around the breakfast table on the Mornington Peninsula. Sure, my face had reddened at Teddy's retelling of my maniac midnight vampire routine, and although there were a few laughs and raised eyebrows, almost everyone in that holiday house made a special effort to talk to me about my night terrors. Some shared stories of people they knew who experienced similar issues. They were all keen to let me know that it was fairly common and no big deal.

When we try to control situations we often have our guard up. We resist interventions from others which could lead to a healthy change of outlook. Whether he knew what he was doing or not, Teddy took it upon himself to force me to confront uncomfortable emotional situations that I was trying to control. He pushed me to become vulnerable. Without his intervention I probably would have kept my proctalgia fugax a tightly held secret, which could quite possibly have made it even worse. (My bottom is fine these days, by the way. Thanks for asking.)

My instinct had been to hide the thing I considered to be a flaw and a weakness – to control my image – but the second I shared it, the anxiety I'd attached to it disappeared. I didn't lose friends because I had proctalgia fugax and no one thought less of me because I had night terrors. Those were my greatest fears, because we all have a strong desire to belong, be part of a group and feel love and connection. As Brené Brown writes, 'Vulnerability sounds like truth and feels like courage. Truth and courage aren't always comfortable, but they're never weakness.'[1]

Being vulnerable doesn't mean we have to get up in front of a football team and tell them our deepest, darkest secrets. Nor does it require a friend to group email your embarrassing condition. You can start small with vulnerability. Perhaps you could journal whatever it is you're struggling with, then work your way up to sharing that journal entry with someone you are close to and whom you trust. It's not something to dive blindly into, but dipping your toe in the water, to courageously speak your truth, will inevitably lead to authentic connection.

This is one of the reasons why, along with two of my favourite people in the world – comedian Ryan Shelton and my brother Josh – I launched *The Imperfects* podcast. The premise was simple: we'd invite outwardly successful and happy people onto the show and ask them to open up about their problems and insecurities. During the editing process, I'd listen to our guests reveal the challenges of their journey, over and over again. Slowly, I began to see where we were all going wrong.

Vulnerability, control and letting go

Vulnerability points us to the universal truth that some things are simply beyond our control. When we try to control the elements of life over which we have no influence, we inevitably end up frustrated, angry, stressed, anxious, depressed and, in my case, with a very sore bottom. The stories above serve not only to illustrate vulnerability but they also remind us of the futility and consequences of trying to do the impossible. As a 24-year-old, I was far too worried about what other people thought of me. It took a while to realise we have no say in what others think of us.

Doggedly trying to exert control affects all aspects of our lives; whether we're fretting about a medical condition and trying to project a certain image, or worrying about death. The most recent example of my attempt to control the uncontrollable arose thanks to COVID-19. It took nineteen months and six lockdowns before I stopped stressing out over the impact the pandemic was having on me and my loved ones. I had grown so frustrated and anxious about the world that I was forced to question exactly what it was that I feared. It was fairly simple: I was scared things would never go back to the way they were. I'd decided my kids were going to endure lockdown for years. They were going to struggle socially. They were going to grow up in a world of masked, isolated people.

Ultimately, by doing the following exercise, I realised the virus was going to do whatever it wanted: history would take its course irrespective of my hand-wringing. I recognised that I needed to let go of the anxiety and accept reality: in other words, I had to surrender control. The second I did this, I felt better. The word 'surrender' quite literally means 'to stop fighting' and the very thought of no longer fighting COVID-19 filled me with an instant sense of calm.

EXERCISE

- Write down all the things that cause you ongoing stress, worry and anxiety.
- Put a line through the things on the list that are out of your control.
- Circle the items you do have control over.
- Devote your energy and concentration to solving the problems in the circles.
- The problems with lines through them are still on the page – they don't go away – but there is nothing you can do to make them change so you just have to let them go.

If any of the remaining problems prove too hard to let go of in that moment, it is worth subjecting them to a four-question process American writer and speaker Byron Katie calls 'doing the work'.[2] In my case, the fear was that COVID-19 had changed the world forever and my children's lives would be adversely and permanently affected. So I 'did the work' and asked myself the following:

1. Is it true?
2. Can you know absolutely that it is true?
3. What happens when you react to this thought?
4. Who would you be without this thought?

My answers:

1. Maybe.
2. Not really.
3. I feel anxious, sad and hopeless.
4. I'd feel like myself again: calm, joyful and full of hope.

I am only too aware that life sometimes hands us circumstances that seem too big or too painful to simply let go of; that no amount of vulnerability or the ceding of control can change. Life's lottery means many people may never feel 'calm, joyful and full of hope'. But I have seen that even in the depths of immense human suffering, letting go of control can alleviate pain. So why not give it a go?

CHAPTER 6

FOR MB

James Macready-Bryan was one of a kind.

Known almost universally as MB, he was one of my brother Josh's best mates growing up and an occasional, cheeky and adorable visitor to our family home. After he left school he played at my football club, where he was a very handy winger despite being the smallest bloke in the team. But what MB lacked in stature he made up for in courage, personality and determination. He was a delightfully naughty kid, who somehow managed to get away with all kinds of mischief thanks to his immense charm and outsized sense of fun.

Josh and his mates loved MB to bits. In Chapter 4
I said I felt like I had lost the ability to light up a room.
Well, MB wrote the book on lighting up a room. He didn't
need to warm up or ease into a social situation, he *was* the
social situation. I can't claim to have been a close friend of
his, but Josh certainly was, and I understood why. In writing this chapter I asked Josh to describe MB before the
incident.

The MB I knew as a teenager was cheeky . . . really
cheeky; he was funny and he was the right amount of
naughty. To be around James was to get carried away
with the joy of the moment. Whether it was playing
some game he'd just made up or sneaking our way
into a six-pack of beer (or some disgusting 'rocket fuel'
concoction), it was always exciting and always fun.
These moments were always punctuated by MB making
a joke or an inappropriate observation followed by
his wide-eyed, wide-mouthed look of shock – a second
of a, 'Did I really just say that' silence, followed by a
loud cackle of laughter often placing a hand on you or
around you in the moment. It was a rare and beautiful
connection between two boys trying to figure out the
world in the funniest way possible. I miss that MB.

Despite being very popular, MB didn't have a girlfriend in Year 10. Back then though his family probably would have told you a different story. This is because MB dreamt up an imaginary girlfriend named Sarah. His mum Robyn was so excited about the lovely development in her son's life that a couple of times when MB said he was going out with Sarah on the weekend, she gave him a fifty dollar note to spend. 'So, when are we going to meet her?' she would ask.

'Oh, we'll have to see, Mum,' MB would reply. 'We're just meeting up at her friend's place tonight.'

MB would skip out the door with fifty bucks in his pocket to bankroll a case of beer and a night hanging out with his mates. Naughty-slash-hilarious. The following year, however, MB landed a real girlfriend and, wouldn't you know it, her name was Sarah. Such was the ridiculousness of life on planet MB.

Our footy club's 2006 presentation was on a Saturday night and happened to coincide with MB's twentieth birthday. I opted to pass on the presentation because I had to play cricket the following day, but MB went for a bit and then took a train into the city to meet up with another group of friends to celebrate the end of his teenage years and the beginning of a long and promising life ahead.

Josh and his mates were at that age when things were starting to fall into place, and MB was no exception. He may have liked to party, but he was very intelligent and ambitious, too. As an arts/law student at Monash University, the world lay at his feet.

Arriving at Flinders Street Station, MB met up with another friend, Adrian, the younger brother of a close mate of mine. They set off into the CBD together. As they walked along Lonsdale Street they exchanged words with a girl walking in the opposite direction. A few minutes later they were confronted by two young men.

'What the fuck did you just say to my girlfriend?' one of them reportedly said.

MB apologised and he and Adrian continued on their way, but shortly afterwards they noticed they were being followed by the same guys. Before they knew it, they were set upon and MB had his head repeatedly bashed into a bluestone wall. A passer-by intervened and told them to run but unfortunately they took a wrong turn and ended up down a dead-end alleyway. Trapped, MB reportedly apologised again and put his hands up in submission. As he did so, he was coward punched in the face. He fell onto the footpath, unconscious.

The next morning I was at Jubilee Oval in Frankston

getting ready for our game when Josh phoned to say he wouldn't be able to play.

'Why mate?' I asked. 'What's up?'

'I got woken by a phone call at six am,' he said quietly. 'MB's been punched and he's in hospital.'

'Shit! That's not good,' I said, taken aback. 'You'd better go and see him.'

'Yeah, but I'm not sure he's conscious. Apparently it might be pretty bad.'

The words 'pretty bad' usually meant a broken nose or maybe some missing teeth. I stayed at cricket all day and wasn't too worried. I didn't hear from Josh and whenever I wondered how things were going I had a mental image of MB sitting up in a hospital bed with a broken jaw or swollen black eyes. Not great thoughts, but I figured he'd be okay. Back then I didn't realise the terrible places a punch in the head could take you to.

At Royal Melbourne Hospital, the reality was horrifying. When Josh arrived, the first thing he noticed was a piece of medical gauze that had been placed across MB's forehead with the words 'NO BONE FLAP' written on it in large, red, capital letters. Anxious to relieve pressure on his dangerously swelling brain, surgeons had been forced to remove a large piece of MB's skull.

The impact of that punch reverberated in concentric circles, like a pebble dropped into a still pond. The waves of grief swept outwards and swamped everyone who loved MB: his family and the large and tight-knit group of friends for whom MB had been a touchstone as they grew up.

When Josh finally arrived home that night and explained how bad things were, I was so shocked I had to go outside on my own to try to process it. I'd seen fights in pubs and nightclubs before, where guys would punch each other in the head for stupid, drunken reasons, but it had never occurred to me it could be potentially fatal or life-altering.

The split second MB hit the ground, life as he knew it was over. He was unrecognisable, he could hardly move and he was unable to communicate. The muscles in his hands and feet curled in spasms, while his voice and quick-witted chat were replaced by heartbreaking and indecipherable grunts.

The two assailants were caught and eventually jailed but there was a powerful feeling among MB's devastated mates that something else needed to come from this tragedy. This wasn't the end of the story. It certainly wasn't the end for MB. Today he is conscious and aware of his surroundings but has very limited communication and is fed through a tube. He requires 24-hour attention in a high-care facility. His amazing mum Robyn, who was a teacher at my school, is never far from his bedside. Robyn was the cool teacher. Everyone wanted to be in her class. But the night her boy was attacked, she became one of those people for whom calmness, joyfulness and a feeling of hope grew elusive.

In the hope of preventing anyone else's family suffering in the same way, MB's friends launched a public education campaign called 'Step Back Think'. The program aims to put an end to social violence by publicising the reality of what can happen when people fight with their fists. I ended up in the role of CEO for a short while. My main task was to visit schools around Victoria to talk to students about the scourge of needless violence in society, especially where alcohol and young men are involved.

I would tell them MB's story and show them a video Josh had created that underscored the enormity of the loss. After a while I couldn't watch it anymore and took to watching the students' reaction instead. The video never failed to move them, and I would often gaze in sadness and hope across a sea of devastated teenage faces.

At first I put this visceral reaction down to the fact that they had empathy for MB and his friends. Perhaps they had someone just like him in their social group. The more I watched their faces, however, the more I sensed their awakening to the fact that nothing is certain in life: awful things beyond our control often happen to good people. We'd show the film to graduating Year 12 students before they headed off for Schoolies week: a notorious time of boozing and risky behaviour.

The most beautiful but also heartbreaking moment while writing this book came from a conversation I had with Robyn. I didn't plan on writing about MB; I just wanted to talk to her about accepting the things we can't control. I wanted to understand if it was possible to do so in the wake of such a tragic event. As we chatted, I realised this was the first conversation I'd had with Robyn in ten years without MB being there. All our conversations had been by his bedside. In those moments, I would see a devoted, compassionate, loving and resilient mother. Now, as we spoke over the phone, I was reminded of the teacher I once knew. Intelligent, insightful, witty and calm. Near the end of our chat, I mentioned the word 'control'.

'One of the most important but toughest things I've had to do for myself is accept the situation,' Robyn told me. 'It has taken me a long time, and I am still so heartbroken, but I cannot control the past, so I had to let it go. The other thing I've learnt is one never truly knows what others are dealing with, which is why we all need to treat each other with respect and kindness. This is something that troubles me – why so many humans can't do this. It's another thing I'm going to have to accept.'

Robyn's honest and measured response to enduring the unimaginable was profoundly moving.

'Robyn, would you be okay with me sharing your story in my book?' I asked nervously.

There was a long pause. Then I heard Robyn crying.

'That would mean so much, Hugh,' she said. 'Please tell people he has endured a huge amount but he still at times shows us his big MB smile and sense of humour. He is fighting for his best life and doing as well as he can. I would love for people to know what James was like before the assault.'

It's a great honour to share MB's story with you here. It is no coincidence that a day after speaking with his mum, I finally decided I had to accept that the COVID-19 pandemic was out of my control. Robyn gave me the strength to finally surrender and let go. So thank you, Robyn, for helping me and for generously allowing me to share your story. I truly hope it will help others.

PERFECTION

CHAPTER 7

ONE (NOT SO) PERFECT DAY

Penny reckoned I looked like I'd seen a ghost as I put my phone down on the kitchen table and stared at her in shock. 'They're going to be here in two minutes!' I gasped.

'Who's going to be here in two minutes?' my wife asked, trepidation suddenly written across her face, too.

'*Missy Higgins!*' I blurted as panic rose in my chest. 'Missy, Dan and the kids are almost here!'

I'm the first to admit I get a bit star-struck from time to time. Ever since I was a kid with posters of Andrew Gaze, Steve Waugh and Jason Dunstall on my wall, I've held my heroes in stratospheric regard, even after I've had the privilege of getting to know a few of them through my work with The Resilience Project. Mostly they're sports stars. Missy Higgins, however, was on another level.

As far as I'm concerned, Missy Higgins is the most loveable Australian music icon of all time (I'm including Jimmy Barnes and John Farnham in that one-person poll). Her award-winning album *The Sound of White* was the soundtrack of my twenties. For a long time, like many Australians, I suspect, I managed to apply the lyrics of 'The Special Two' to every romantic situation I found myself in. 'This song is totally about us,' I'd coo, way too often. And, yes, like everyone else who said that to a love interest, I felt silly when I discovered the song wasn't about a romantic partner at all. Yep, I'd been a massive Missy fan for a long time. And now she was about to walk through our front door.

Some background: Missy and her husband Dan came to one of my talks in Melbourne a few years ago. When my first book was due to be published in 2019, without knowing her that well, I made contact and asked whether she'd consider providing a testimonial. To my astonishment she said yes.

Fast forward a year and I invited her to appear on *The Imperfects* to hopefully open up about the struggles in her life. Again, amazingly, she said yes and, after a fairly intense and personal interview, our association grew into a friendship. It turned out Missy and her husband Dan have children around the same ages as ours. Before too long, our families started spending time together.

When you're slogging through the trenches of toddlerhood the chance to share the foxhole with another couple who are also under siege from outrageous little humans is a great boost to your sanity. War stories are told, notes are compared and strong bonds are forged by the blowtorch of battle.

Missy and Dan are such a down-to-earth couple that you never feel like you're in the presence of musical greatness. That said, I still put myself under ridiculous pressure to make sure everything was perfect on the day they were due to come to our place for the first time. I'd drafted a long list of things that I needed to make sure were perfect, beginning, naturally enough, with what music we should play.

Like a Hollywood director I agonised over the perfect soundtrack to this great meeting of families. I lost sleep over it and even fretted about the teenage girls next door who were partial to playing Missy Higgins records at volume.

'What if they put on her music while she's here?' I asked Penny on the eve of the big day. 'Do you think I should go next door and ask the girls not to play any of her records tomorrow?'

My hand-wringing rubbed off on Penny, too. 'Oh my God, what music *do* you put on when Missy Higgins is coming over?' she wondered out loud.

'I honestly don't know. Do you think we should have one of her songs playing as she's walking in?'

'Oh my God, no,' she said, 'that would be extremely odd.'

In the end, Penny came up with a safe solution. She downloaded a playlist from Spotify that would hopefully give us the appearance of being cool: some pleasant sonic wallpaper to our family afternoon. Finally I was able to cross the most pressing item off my catalogue of things to obsess over.

It was winter and I'd hit upon the great idea of buying an outdoor fire pit specially for the occasion. In my mind I pictured us having a couple of beers around the fire pit while the kids played beautifully together and smooth tunes hummed out of the speakers. It promised to be a perfect afternoon.

Since we have artificial grass in our backyard I figured I'd need to put something underneath the fire pit to stop it damaging the 'lawn' and made a mental note to grab some leftover pavers we had lying around in the garage. For the time being, though, I just plonked the thing down on the artificial grass and went inside to fixate over the finer details of nibbles and drinks.

It was then that my phone vibrated with an incoming message:

'Hey Hugh. We're running really early. Be there soon. Missy.'

What?! Who runs half an hour early?

I couldn't believe what was happening. I raced around the house frantically trying to make sure everything was just so. I'd really wanted the fire pit to look warm and welcoming (i.e. on fire) when they walked in, so I quickly threw some kindling and logs in, set it alight and went back inside.

'Okay, I think we're sorted,' I said to Penny as we waited for a knock at the door. At the same moment, we both realised the Spotify playlist had conjured up a Missy Higgins song, which now filled the house.

'Oh my God! Turn it off. Turn it *off! Quick!*' I yelped as Penny lunged at her phone and pulled the plug on what would have been the awkward suburban coronation of Missy Higgins. For all our preoccupation with getting the music just right, the house was silent when our guests arrived, arms full of children and bags brimming with bibs, wipes and bottles – the very un-rock'n'roll accoutrement of parenthood.

'Oh *heyyy*, come on in, guys,' I said, as if I'd just remembered they were coming over. 'How are you going? Come out the back, we're just hanging out by the fire.'

Missy and Dan are laid-back parents but even they seemed a bit concerned about their kids, aged five and two, being anywhere near my open-air inferno. 'Sure,' Dan said as we wandered outside, 'we can stand around a fire pit if you want. Are the kids going to be okay with this going on?'

Shit, my inner voice scolded me. I didn't think this through. Luna, their two-year-old, was running around curiously investigating everything, as was our daughter Elsie. Instead of chilling over beers by the fire, we were in a state of high alert, shuffling from side to side, arms outstretched like premier league goalkeepers, trying to stop the kids from getting burnt. Oh Jesus, I thought as I took it all in. What was I thinking?

We eventually managed to steer the little people towards the trampoline and out of harm's way. Things settled down for a while and our three-year-old son Benji hit it off beautifully with their little boy, Sammy, age five.

After a while the boys disappeared into the house and I noticed their squeals had fallen silent. It transpired that Benji had gone to the toilet – something he had recently mastered – and Sammy had very generously followed him into the loo to coach him through it. I heard part of the exchange through the closed door when I went to check on them.

'Is it coming out yet?' Sammy asked.

'No,' Benji replied, 'but it's on its way. Hold on.'

'Okay,' Sammy said. 'That's good. Keep trying.'

It sounded like they had it covered so I left them to it and went back outside to join Penny, Missy and Dan by the fire. We were just starting to settle into a nice little rhythm as we laughed about the coaching session that was unfolding upstairs when Dan said, 'I can smell plastic burning. Can you smell that?'

'Yeah, there's definitely plastic burning somewhere,' Missy concurred after giving the air an exploratory sniff. 'I can totally smell it.'

I could smell it, too, and I knew it was from my synthetic lawn that was starting to melt because I had placed a giant steel bowl full of burning logs directly on top of it.

'Nah, it's probably nothing,' I assured them, nonchalantly nursing my beer and praying the smell would just go away. 'It's fine!'

It wasn't fine, of course. The fucking grass was on fire. We ended up having to douse it in water and retreat inside to escape the noxious miasma of steam and smoke that had enveloped the yard.

Back in the safety of the house we were surprised to discover the boys were still in the bathroom where Sammy was continuing to call the plays. Benji was almost done, so the boys were having a bit of a 'post-match' discussion, summarising the events that had just transpired. Again, I heard all this through the door, and as much as I was loving the guidance and mentoring, I suggested Sammy unlock it so I could help Benji.

Unfortunately Sammy couldn't figure out how the lock worked and with Benji marooned on the toilet, they suddenly realised they were trapped. The coaching session unravelled as the boys started to freak out. There were a few cries for help before I finally coached the coach and his protégé on how to unlock the door.

Free at last, the boys scurried off to play in the garage and I was free to play host again. After a while, though, I thought I'd better go and check on them.

'Do you really think the garage is the best place to be playing, fellas?' I asked as I stepped inside.

'This isn't the garage,' Benji said with a giggle. 'This is the silly house.'

'Yeah, it's the silly house,' Sammy chimed in. 'You can only be in here if you're silly.'

'Yeah, do your really silly dancing, Daddy!' pleaded Benji.

I couldn't handle the thought of letting Benji down in front of his new friend. 'Okay,' I agreed reluctantly, 'here it comes.' As I threw myself all over the garage, Benji looked at Sammy as if to say, I told you it was silly. Sammy nodded his approval, as if to say, Yeah, it's pretty silly. The boys (myself included) were loving it; we laughed and squealed, and pretty soon there was a faint knock at the door.

'Ooh, I wonder if someone else wants to come into the silly house,' I said and flung the door open with gusto, just like a court jester. Bang! The door hit little Luna flush in the face. The poor girl was knocked flat on her back where she lay screaming.

I stood there open-mouthed in disbelief and still clinging to the door handle as Missy swooped in from the lounge room to scoop Luna up and soothe her. What is *wrong* with me? I thought as every turn seemed to bring with it more mayhem.

Missy and Dan, however, were completely cool about the rolling chaos of the afternoon. They stuck around for hours – long after we thought they'd want to get the hell away from us – and remained warm, charming and understanding throughout. This clearly wasn't the first time they'd seen action on the front line.

It was well after dark when they eventually left, although Dan first had to chase Sammy down the street because the little guy didn't want to go home. After they climbed into the car and their tail lights disappeared around the corner, I turned to Penny and smiled sheepishly. 'I don't think they'll want to hang out with us again,' I said.

'You had a shocker,' she said, laughing.

'I know,' I agreed, rubbing a thumb and forefinger into my furrowed brow.

Later that night I received a long message from Missy saying they'd had the most wonderful time catching up. I knew that Sammy had enjoyed himself (probably because I hadn't slammed him in the face with a door) but it was the complete opposite of how I'd expected Missy and Dan would feel about the day.

It took a little while for the penny to drop. I had invested so much emotional capital in trying to make the occasion perfect that I couldn't appreciate all the great things that were happening right in front of me. The *imperfections* made it a memorable day. The screw-ups, the shortfalls and the embarrassing dropped balls brought us closer together. I wouldn't even be writing about it here if the day had been 'perfect'. Most likely I'd have forgotten about much of it.

The fact I had literally set my backyard on fire, locked their son in a toilet and flattened their baby girl was where the beauty lay. These were the things we bonded over and where connections were made. So, too, was the freaking out with Penny over music and Dan trying to catch little Sammy at the end of the visit. None of it perfect, all of it wonderful, all of it connecting.

This may have been obvious to Missy and Dan, and maybe even to you, but to me it was a timely reminder. The truth is I had spent much of my life setting myself up to fail by striving for different kinds of perfection. In focusing on idealised goals I missed out on the really good stuff that happens.

For years I would conduct harsh post-mortems on every public talk I gave the moment I got offstage. If I didn't think it was perfect I'd feel very low and critical of myself. I think this comes from many years playing sport, where you meticulously analyse all that you did wrong after every match in order to improve.

The same went for media interviews. I once made the mistake of listening back to an appearance I'd made on Osher Günsberg's podcast, *Better Than Yesterday*. At the time I thought it had gone swimmingly, but on review I zeroed in on several moments I decided didn't measure up to 'perfect' and was bummed for days. Even when I was out running and my times were slightly down on the previous session I'd get annoyed with myself. Don't even get me started on the front lawn! It's actual grass, and if it wasn't constantly groomed to a showroom state of verdant perfection I'd feel very disappointed.

Worse than that, perfectionism also put walls up around me. If I didn't feel on top of the world I simply wouldn't answer my phone – even the calls from people I loved – for fear I wouldn't be able to produce 'perfect chat' in that moment. My measurement of perfection wasn't purely based on my own subjective standards, either. I could just as easily be swayed by others, even perfect strangers.

In 2018 I delivered what I felt was a perfect talk at the Convention Centre in Melbourne. I was basking in the afterglow the following day when I opened an email from someone who actually hadn't been at the talk, but had sent some of their colleagues along. It was a very considered dot-point breakdown criticising me and my material. Boom! Gutted. Head in hands. The timing could not have been worse. Or, as it turned out, better.

I had just sat down at a quiet cafe in Hawthorn ahead of my first meeting with professional mentor and leadership coach Ben Crowe. I'd read a bit about Ben in the media and knew he worked with Pete Sampras, Andre Agassi and Tiger Woods, among others. Dustin Martin from the Richmond Football Club arranged for me to meet Ben in person.

While I was excited about the catch-up I was a little wary, too. I've often been disappointed upon meeting people who worked in the same field. There are a lot of big egos afoot and many see the education and wellbeing space as a competitive arena. As I put my phone away in anticipation of Ben's arrival, I willed myself to forget about the devastating email that sat like a layer of poison at the top of my inbox.

Ben turned out to be the opposite of my worst fears. He was warm, genuine and sincerely interested. We played a long game of conversational table tennis as we tried to swat the focus off of ourselves and onto the other.

'So, how was your talk last night?' Ben asked, focusing on a topic I couldn't easily whack back at him.

'If you'd asked me that thirty minutes ago I would have said it was perfect,' I said.

Ben looked surprised. 'What on earth happened thirty minutes ago to change that?'

I told him about the email and, without realising it, stepped straight through the door of his wheelhouse. Ben leant across the table, grabbed hold of my jumper, pulled me in close and said, 'You are worthy of love, Hugh.'

'Sorry?' I said, a little flustered.

'You are worthy of love and belonging – just as you are,' he repeated. 'Yes, you're imperfect and, yes, you're full of struggles, but you are worthy – just as you are.'

It was a pretty full-on offering and I didn't know how to respond, so I just let the words sink in. One landed with particular resonance: 'imperfect'.

'Yeah, I'm imperfect,' I finally said in a small voice.

'We all are!' Ben jumped in. 'Life is imperfect, but that's where the beauty lies. Imperfections connect us. We *bond* over our imperfections.'

Ben explained to me how I'd been attaching my self-worth to my talks. If I did a great job, I felt like people would like me. If people didn't like what I had to say or how I said it, I believed they didn't like me. Perfectionism, he said, had control over my life. In a way, I already knew it.

PERFECTIONISM

Perfectionism is defined as a personality trait where we make overly critical self-evaluations and impose excessively high standards on ourselves, on others, or both. When it's directed inwardly, perfectionism causes us to place irrational importance on being 'perfect'. When we fall short – as we almost always do – we see ourselves as failures. Simply put, perfectionism is a circular psychological struggle we can never win.

Perfectionism is nothing new to humanity, but it is on the rise. A 2019 study by Thomas Curran from the University of Bath and Andrew P. Hill from York St John University looked at the increasing rates of perfectionism reported by university students over past generations. They noted a correlation between neoliberal governments in the US, the UK and Canada (and you could safely add Australia) since the 1980s that emphasised 'competitive individualism'. In response, they said, people agitated 'to perfect themselves and their lifestyles'.

Curran and Hill's landmark study found the average university student in 2016 was up to 33 per cent more likely to have perfectionistic tendencies than undergraduates in the 1990s.

Nowadays, 'as many as two in five kids and adolescents are perfectionists', according to Katie Rasmussen, who researches child development and perfectionism at West Virginia University. 'It's heading toward an epidemic and public health issue.'

The consequences of perfectionism aren't confined to the self-defeating treadmill of chasing unattainable standards: they can also be debilitating and deadly. Studies have linked perfectionism to clinical problems ranging from depression and anxiety to obsessive-compulsive disorder, chronic fatigue, insomnia, eating disorders and suicide.

There are three common types of perfectionism:

- Self-oriented – when we demand perfection from ourselves.
- Other-oriented – when we expect perfection from people around us.
- Socially prescribed – when we feel pressure from the world around us to be perfect.

Nothing encapsulates the brutal external forces of socially prescribed perfectionism better than platforms like Facebook, Instagram and TikTok. Social media (as well as traditional media) dispenses a torrent of curated 'perfection' every second of every day and night. We carry society's ideal of perfection around in our pockets and check in with it, on average, eighty-five times a day! Our kids' lives are awash with these signals more than at any other time in history – no wonder Katie Rasmussen says we're on the verge of an epidemic.

If, like me, you are among the growing number of people with perfectionistic tendencies, you are definitely up against it. So it is most definitely time to let go. A 2018 study led by Dr Madeleine Ferrari at the Australian Catholic University found that practising self-compassion helped protect people with perfectionistic tendencies against depression.[3]

Self-compassion is the willingness to be kind and forgiving to one's self and to lower standards that are unreasonable: to reset our inner dialogue, in other words. Once again a psychologist, counsellor or therapist can help with this but you could just as easily begin by discussing perfectionism with a friend or family member.

A useful exercise is to simply write down a list of all the areas of your life where you are striving for perfection. For me, the list reads: front lawn (yes, really), running, abs, cleanliness of kitchen and living room, and quality of phone calls.

Once you have written your list, answer the following question: What would happen if these individual items weren't perfect? For me, the answer is 'absolutely nothing'. Nothing would happen. What I have come to realise through this exercise is that my desire to 'create perfect' is completely irrational.

I was lucky that I just stumbled into my conversation with Ben Crowe. As our talk meandered through other topics that day I found myself mentally returning time and again to the word 'imperfection' – a powerful new term in my inner conversation.

'I need to let go of perfection!' I suddenly blurted while Ben was talking about something else.

'Oh, we all do, mate,' he said with a smile. 'You're not alone.'

Over the following months I made a concerted effort to practise self-compassion. 'I'm imperfect!' became a mantra I'd whisper to myself throughout the day. To begin with, it gave me permission to forgive myself if I didn't do something perfectly, but over time it made me realise I'd been way too harsh on myself for way too long.

While we can't all sit down for a coffee one on one with Ben, he has developed a great app called Mojo Crowe that I highly recommend. It's a mindset course that is designed to help you own your story.

In the three years since I changed my perfectionistic inner dialogue through self-compassion I have felt happier and more relaxed. In work, family life, my social circle and inside my own head, the expectation I have is to do my best. I no longer take criticism to heart and I no longer feel the pressure of a world ruled by the internet to be perfect. Hell, I don't even mind that I burnt a hole in the grass.

CHAPTER 8

TEACHING THE TEACHER

I've often wondered what became of Australia's squash courts. The sport was fairly popular for much of the twentieth century and when I was growing up every second suburb had a squash centre equipped with an outrageously good canteen and an arcade game, usually *Space Invaders*. But by the turn of the millennium we seemed to have thrown away our racquets and abandoned the game forever. In 2010, though, I discovered at least one of Melbourne's forgotten squash courts had been reborn and converted into a thoroughly bizarre teaching space.

In my second year working at SEDA College teaching adolescent students who were disengaged with traditional schooling, I was told my new classroom would be in the sports centre at Melbourne University. I was pumped about teaching on the fabled campus until I discovered I'd be doing so in a converted squash court. If that wasn't weird enough, the side walls of the court had been covered in gigantic mirrors.

To access this 'classroom' we had to walk down a dark tunnel, past five other abandoned courts. Once inside – where desks and chairs had been neatly arrayed – I had to teach twenty-eight students aged 17 to 19 as we all did our best not to stare into the mirrors and lose ourselves in thousands of diminishing reflections. The place felt more like an asylum or a laboratory than a classroom. This was early on in SEDA's programming; they have fantastic facilities now.

Fortunately, the students were a great bunch of kids. One of my favourites was a young man named Matthew Lanigan. A gifted footballer and cricketer, Matt had moved to Melbourne from Swan Hill in northern Victoria to be part of the SEDA program. Since it was his first time out of the nest – not to mention living in a big city on his own – I promised his parents, Gerald and Sue, that I'd keep an eye out for their beloved boy.

Matt and I hit it off instantly. He played grade cricket in the same competition as I did so we always had a lot to talk about.

Having come from the country to the big smoke, Matt could have been forgiven for being a little reclusive, but he was the opposite. Warm, personable, engaging and very funny, Matt managed to allocate a nickname to everyone in the class and always made a point of bringing everyone into his conversations. His energy and passion for life were impossible to resist. His classmates loved him as much as I did.

Now and then he'd stick around in our high-walled mirrored cube after school to shoot the breeze and exchange notes on life with me. One afternoon, as we chatted away and chipped a football to each other from opposite ends of the court/classroom, Matt went strangely quiet. A bit nonplussed, I kicked the ball to him. Instead of kicking it back, he held it in one hand as his shoulders slumped and his head dropped.

'Ah . . . what are you doing?' I asked. I didn't understand what had come over him. He was acting weird, as if someone had just whispered an instruction into his ear to do an impersonation of someone feeling sad, like a pantomime.

'Seriously, mate, what are you doing?' I asked again.

After a few long seconds Matt lifted his head and looked me straight in the eye. 'I don't feel right.'

'Don't feel right in what way?' I said, still confused. 'Are you feeling sick?'

Matt shook his head. 'I don't know what it is,' he murmured. 'I just don't feel very happy at the moment.'

This was the last thing I expected to hear. It didn't compute. Here was the brightest spark in my class who, seconds beforehand, had been playfully passing the footy, sharing outrageous anecdotes about his mates back home. Now it seemed like his inner light had been suddenly switched off. While I'd had some experience of living with someone with a mental illness, I was by no means an expert. I didn't know what to make of this sudden reversal of mood in my little mate or, crucially, what to do about it.

'I'm sorry, Matty, but I don't really follow what you're saying,' I said.

With that he dropped the football and with his arms hanging limply by his side, he began to cry. I wish I could say that I walked over to him in that moment, wrapped an arm around his shoulders and tried to comfort him. But I didn't. I froze and stayed right where I was, ten metres away on the other side of the room.

Meanwhile, what had begun as heartbreaking whimpers

had grown into terrible howls of pain that wracked Matt's body. The poor kid was trying to tell me something but he couldn't get the words out.

Still stuck in my no man's land of total incomprehension, I could only muster a variation of the same dumb question, 'Are you okay, mate?'

Matt then started getting really anxious. He gulped in mouthfuls of air and looked frightened. I'd never witnessed a panic attack before and I wondered whether he might be having one. It was that thought that finally snapped me out of my daze. I hurried over and put an arm around him. He clung on to me as if I were a lifejacket and his boat was sinking.

Eventually I managed to sit him down. As we slumped side by side with our backs against a massive mirror, Matt started to get his breath back. 'I don't know why but I just feel so sad all the time,' he finally croaked through the tears. 'I don't want to come to school – ever. It's a real struggle. I can hardly get out of bed in the morning.'

I'd noticed Matt had been arriving at school a little late for a week or so, but I put it down to teenage tardiness or maybe problems with public transport. I was still trying to think of how to respond to what he'd said when he lifted his chin and stared into the endless reflections of himself. 'I think I might have that depression thing,' he said flatly.

Now that I knew what the problem was, I found myself embarrassingly unequipped to handle it. Having never had any training – formal or otherwise – in how to respond in such a situation with a student, I made a terrible mistake. Upon hearing Matt's cry for help I inadvertently handed the problem straight back to him.

'What do you want to do?' I said.

'I want to go home,' he sobbed. 'I want to go back to Swan Hill.'

'Okay, I think getting you home is a good idea,' I said. 'I'll ring your dad.'

A minute or so later I was on the phone to Gerald, doing my best to explain what was happening. He said they'd drop everything and come straight away. I stayed with Matt for the next few hours as his parents made the long drive south. He wept for almost every minute. With nothing else to offer, all I could do was sit with him.

It was dark when Gerald and Sue arrived. They seemed as shocked and as thrown as I'd been about the emotional state of their usually happy and upbeat son. 'Maybe he's just really tired,' I offered weakly.

'Yeah, maybe,' Gerald said as he put his arm around his boy. 'I think we'd best get you home, mate.'

'Please let me know how he's going,' I asked as they left. 'And tell me if there's anything I can do to help.'

The following morning my phone rang at 6.30. It was Gerald. He'd just found Matt hanging in their garage.

'He's alive, thank God,' the poor man cried into the phone. 'I was able to get him down.'

Overcome with shock and sadness, I dropped the phone. Matt was in a stable condition and on his way to the Melbourne Clinic, a leading mental health facility in Richmond. 'We'll be there in a couple of hours, too,' Gerald said. 'Do you think you could come by, Hugh?'

I phoned the school as soon as I could to let them know what had happened, and that I'd be at the Melbourne Clinic for the morning. When I arrived, Matt was sitting up in a bed, cloaked in a hoodie, as if hiding from the world behind a fabric barricade. He refused to look at me. By the time I left later that day he still hadn't said a word to me.

For the next two months I went to the clinic after school every day to visit Matt for an hour or so. I'd relay news from the classroom and give him some schoolwork to look at – anything to push suicide ideation out of his head. 'Everyone at school misses you, Matty,' I'd say.

But he still wouldn't speak.

Back in class I had to have a frank conversation with

the other students. It was hard to know how much to tell them but I figured they were all on the brink of adulthood so I decided I should treat them accordingly.

'Matty's in a really bad way,' I explained. 'He's got depression and he's had some pretty bad thoughts about taking his life.'

The kids were wonderful. Every single one responded with compassion. Almost all of them said they wanted to go and visit Matt – but only if it would help.

After a week or so in the clinic, Matt seemed to be in a better place. I asked Gerald and Sue and staff at the clinic what they thought about some of his friends paying a visit. They agreed it was a good idea, but only if Matt was happy to see them.

That afternoon I dropped by on my way home and asked Matt if he'd like some visitors. He shrugged and then nodded his silent consent. The following Monday I arrived at the clinic with a handful of his mates. When I opened the door, however, I was horrified to see the left side of his face covered in deep, bloody scratches.

Shocked, and not knowing how to react, the kids did their best to stay positive. It turned out Matt had taken a dark turn over the weekend and had torn at his own face. I regretted the visit straight away. I felt helpless against his invisible enemy and that my turning up day after day was achieving very little. But I didn't know what else to do.

Knowing Matt was a huge Richmond supporter and that my brother Josh was old schoolmates with the popular Tigers midfielder Daniel Jackson, I organised a visit. Daniel is a big-hearted man and he was terrific with Matt. He arrived at the clinic with an Xbox under his arm and proceeded to set it up in the room before Matt even had a chance to register that he was in the presence of one of his heroes.

'I love my Xbox,' Daniel said to Matt. 'If it's okay with you I'm just gonna leave it here for the time being. If I ever want to play, I'll be heading straight over here, to play with you.'

Matt nodded, and very nearly smiled.

Over the next month Daniel stopped by the clinic every few days to do battle on the Xbox with Matt. It definitely had an impact on his disposition but Daniel felt he could offer more.

During one of my after-school visits it was clear Matt didn't feel up to chatting. 'If you don't want to talk that's fine,' I'd always say. 'I'm just gonna stick around for a while anyway, if that's okay with you.'

Matt never once asked me to leave or told me to stop coming, so I took it that he wanted me there. He was sitting up in bed with his headphones on, listening to music and staring off into nowhere when there were two sharp knocks on the door. Matt didn't hear it but I looked up to see a very familiar and very famous face lean into the room. It was Ben Cousins – premiership-winning West Coast Eagles super-star and celebrated Brownlow medallist. 'Is there a massive legend in here?' Ben asked, grinning. Taken aback, I said, 'Yep!' and shot my hand up. I instantly realised he wasn't asking about me and quickly put my hand back down, feeling like an idiot.

I had no idea, but Daniel Jackson had contacted Ben in the hope of turning things around with Matt. At that time, Ben had been attracting negative headlines for various issues linked to recreational drug use. He knew exactly what it was like to struggle with seemingly insurmountable problems. So it turned out he was the perfect person to visit Matt.

I elbowed Matt. 'Ay, Matty! You've got a visitor.' When Matt saw the living legend walk into the room he whipped his headphones off, smiled widely and said, 'G'day Cuz!' as if they were old friends. I asked Matt if he wanted me to leave.

'Nah, you can stick around,' he said – the first words he'd said to me since the fateful day in our mirrored cube.

'Who's this bloke?' Ben asked loudly, pointing at me.

'Oh, he's my teacher,' said Matt.

'What's he doing here?'

Matt didn't answer, he just stared in awe at Ben. I chose to stay. I didn't want to miss out on Matt's beautiful smile.

It's no secret Ben Cousins has had his problems but that day I saw a man overflowing with empathy. He immediately went to work making Matt feel comfortable, safe, understood and respected – like they were in the same grim fight together.

'So, what drugs have they got you on, Matty?' was his opening gambit.

Matt rattled off the name of the medication his psychiatrist had prescribed.

'Oh, I've been on those, mate,' Ben replied, nodding sagely. 'You know, it's important that you do what the doctors say, okay? I've been to some really dark places before, as you've probably read, but I promise you this – if you put the work in, it's all going to be worth it. You will get through this but it's not just going to happen for you – you've *gotta* put the work in. And just looking at you now, I can see you're the kind of bloke who will.'

Ben stayed with Matt for more than an hour. After about ten minutes I decided to leave them alone. They didn't seem to notice as I made my way to the door. From out in the hallway I could hear laughter, which made me smile but it also brought a tear. I'm not sure what caused the sweaty eyes. Relief perhaps, maybe even gratitude.

An immediate change came over Matt that day. I believe it was a major turning point in his life: a crossroads presented to him by a voice of experience he knew he could trust. What's more, Ben didn't tell him which way to go, he just empowered him to choose the right path.

At the time of writing, Ben Cousins is still in a pretty dark place. He's hunted by the media, he's often in trouble and a lot of people have a very low opinion of him. But the man I met that day in the Melbourne Clinic was as good as a guardian angel, and I will be forever grateful for what he did for Matt.

Ben was right, though. Matt *did* have to put the work in. He had ups and downs on the road to recovery but he faced it all with courage, and with his beautiful parents by his side. When he was discharged from the Melbourne Clinic after two months Matt decided it was best for him to leave SEDA College and return to Swan Hill with his family. Today he's in a great place. I've often wished that Ben Cousins knew this. I'm not sure if Cuz would even remember visiting Matty that day, but something makes me feel like it would do him good to know the incredible impact he had. Matt is a successful greyhound trainer now, based in Geelong. Not only is he successful professionally, but he's also very happy in his life.

When I look back I feel sick to think I was never given mental health training while studying to be a teacher. Had I been, I might have helped ensure the situation with Matt didn't escalate as it did. When somebody reaches out to you and says they're depressed, the first thing you're meant to do (according to guidelines from Mental Health First Aid Australia) is ask, 'Have you thought about killing yourself?'

It's a very hard question but you need to ask it. If the answer is 'yes', you need to follow up with another tough question: 'Have you thought about how you're going to do it?'

When people get to the point of admitting they've thought about suicide and how they'd go about it, it's often a sign they desperately want assistance *not* to do it. It's a cry for help, in other words. I'll never know the answer but I often wonder if I'd asked those questions of Matt, whether he'd have said 'yes' and 'I've thought about ending it in the garage at Mum and Dad's place'.

Had he said that, I'd have been able to involve his parents

immediately and discuss what steps to take next to protect him. For a long time I felt a sense of failure around what happened. I had mismanaged the situation because I was unprepared and unskilled when it came to mental health intervention. It was a major blow to my perfectionistic mind-set. When Matt was getting ready to leave the clinic, Gerald walked me to my car and said, 'You've been so helpful, Hugh, what you've done means so much to our family.' I thanked him, but as I got in my car and drove away, I felt like a fraud.

As in just about every other aspect of my life, I had wanted to be the perfect teacher. True to form, I set my expectations ridiculously high from the start. In fact, I chose the profession not so much to be an educator, but because I wanted to protect young people from the ravages of mental illness. I had seen what it did to my little sister and lived through the effects it had on our family. If I was at the coalface as a teacher, perhaps I could make a difference.

The spectre of suicide had always appalled me – particularly among the young. It's an issue that has only grown worse since I started teaching. The World Health Organization estimated that in 2015, fifteen years after I started out in the classroom, around 788,000 people died by suicide worldwide. That's a staggering number. Many more tried but survived. Suicide accounted for nearly 1.5 per cent of all deaths globally that year, placing it among the twenty leading causes of mortality. In the same year it was the second leading cause of death among 15–29-year-olds.[1]

I had always thought that if I could save just one child or one family from the pain of mental illness – let alone a suicide attempt – I would have justified my career decision. But when the moment came in that ridiculous squash court classroom, the perfectionist within declared I was an abject failure. It was a shame and burden I carried around for years, right up until my meeting with Ben Crowe at that cafe in Hawthorn.

We are not perfect. We make mistakes. We need to forgive ourselves and lower the standards we set for ourselves, and recognise the great paradox of perfectionism is that it stops us from improving. How can we grow if we only admonish ourselves for our shortcomings? How do we evolve if we don't first own our mistakes and then learn from them?

Don't just take it from the experts, take it from me: show yourself some compassion. Speak to yourself the same way you would speak to someone you love. As Ben Crowe says, 'You are worthy of love and belonging – just as you are.'

FEAR OF FAILURE

CHAPTER 9

GEAR-STICKING HAMISH BLAKE

Hamish Blake and Andy Lee are, in my opinion, Australia's greatest ever comedy duo. To say those guys were a staple of my life during my twenties and thirties would be an understatement. I felt a sort of half-removed kinship with them, too: they're around my age, we grew up in the same Melbourne suburbs and their humour could not be a closer match to mine. They look for the best in Australians and share their observations in the most authentic way. No one is ever stung by a punchline in their victimless brand of hilarity. My favourite thing about Hamish and Andy, however, is that they simply spread joy.

Due largely to his frequent references to cricket and his grateful disposition, Hamish always struck me as someone I'd get along with famously. His vibe is so approachable and disarming that I was convinced he'd 'get' me straight away should we ever happen to meet, which I often thought was destined to happen. For most of my thirties we lived in the same suburb and I'd see him out and about. Any time there was a 'Hamish sighting' I'd start coaching myself: 'If you end up chatting to him, be cool and be funny.' I was sure that if I played it right, friendship would ensue.

One Friday, Josh and I were having breakfast at our favourite cafe in inner-city Fitzroy. It was around 7.30 am and the joint was fairly empty so I took notice when there was a bustling at the cafe door. My jaw almost hit the floor when Hamish Blake walked in. At this point Josh had no inkling of my unfulfilled bromance, so what happened next took him by surprise.

'Psst!' I hiss-whispered across the table. Josh's head was buried in the newspaper. 'Check it out!'

'What?' he said, not even bothering to look up.

'Hamish Blake's here!' I whispered a little louder.

'Sorry? Who's here?' he said, screwing up his nose.

'Hamish Blake,' I repeated in what a primary school-teacher would call my 'outside voice'.

At that moment, Hamish walked past our table. He paused, looked at us and smiled. 'Yes, I am!' he said, giving two thumbs up before walking to a table nearby.

'Oh shit,' I berated myself, but I was too excited to leave things alone or behave like a normal person. It was a small cafe and since Hamish was quite close by I realised if I tilted my head, I could overhear the chatter from his table.

'Mate, would you please stop doing that?' Josh said when he saw me eavesdropping.

'But I can hear everything he's saying!' I whispered back.

'Yeah, that's the point,' Josh responded. 'It's very creepy. Please stop it.'

I'd war-gamed this moment plenty of times. After a few minutes of working up the nerve, I told Josh what I was about to do. 'There's no one else here,' I said. 'I'm going to introduce myself very quickly, just to say hi.'

'Oh, please don't do that,' he implored, but I was already getting out of my chair.

'Back in a sec,' I said.

A few years earlier – after The Resilience Project started to get traction in Australian schools – I did my first-ever television interview. I'd been invited to talk about gratitude, empathy and mindfulness on Channel Nine's *Today Show*, but as soon as I sat down opposite the co-host, Georgie Gardiner, disaster struck. I knew what I wanted to say – I'd been talking on the subject for years – but an overwhelming fear of failure had fried the signal between my brain and my mouth. When Georgie posed her first question I froze. Terrified and dumbstruck. On live TV. Right around the country.

Now, as I sidled up to Hamish's table it happened again: my mouth went dry, my palms became sweaty and my heart rate doubled. I just knew I was going to bomb in front of one of my heroes. I'd planned to say something like, 'G'day Hamish! I just wanted to say I love what you do, mate.' But instead I stared at him in silent paralysis, fear etched on my face. It must have been very unsettling for him but, to his credit, he looked up at me with a smile and said, 'G'day mate. How are you going?'

He might as well have been Georgie Gardiner. When I tried to reply I let out a short, high-pitched squeak. With the patience of a saint, Hamish kept smiling. 'Right,' he said. 'Can I help you?'

I responded with two more squeaks as my inner voice desperately tried to take control. You're failing. You look like an idiot, it barked. Say something cool or do something cool right now!

Since speaking seemed not to be an option at that moment, I thought putting my hands on my hips might make me at least appear cool, and maybe even help me relax enough to start using actual words. Because of nerves, brought on by the fear of making an even bigger fool of myself, I couldn't even put my hands on my hips properly. Instead of resting them on my belt line, my thumbs drifted up on either side of my ribcage – not quite under my armpits, but close enough to a chicken impersonation to be very weird.

At last, my outer voice decided to show up. 'Mate – I love your show,' I gushed. 'I love . . . yeah, I love . . . I think you're great. And, so I just . . . yeah! Oh, and Andy! How about Andy? He seems like a lovely, lovely man. Anyway, I hope you have a nice coffee or a nice breakfast, or whatever you're going to have.'

A glance at Josh revealed he was watching through the cracks in his fingers. 'Right, okay,' I said, returning my gaze to a – remarkably – still smiling Hamish Blake. 'I'm going to leave now.'

Before he could respond I abruptly turned and walked back to our table feeling two feet tall. Just as I was about to sit down, Hamish called out, 'Hey mate!'

I spun around as if yanked by an invisible leash. 'Yes?'

'Did you want to do a high five or something?' he asked.

Josh cut in before I could answer. 'No, no, no. Please sit down!'

Not a chance. I went back to Hamish's table as if summoned by the Pope. 'I'd love to do a high five,' I said.

The next few seconds happened in that ultra slow motion people describe after they survive a car accident. As Hamish began to extend his right palm up towards me, I commenced the same action with my right hand. As I did so, my inner voice yapped at me again: This is your chance. Do something cool. Do a *fist bump*. Instead of maintaining an open palm, I curled my fingers into a fist and continued the trajectory towards Hamish's palm.

As Hamish realised I was now positioning for a fist bump, he corrected his hand mid-journey, turning his high five into a fist too in order to meet my knuckles in an explosion of cool. Unfortunately, my brain had belatedly registered Hamish had led with an open palm and, at the same time he was forming a fist, inner-Hugh screamed, Revert to high five! Revert to high five!

The result? I high fived Hamish Blake's fist with my sweaty palm. Josh groaned, but I wasn't done with the weirdness just yet. In an attempt to save the situation I tried to turn the hot mess into a handshake by gripping Hamish's fist and shaking his arm up and down.

It was awkward even for me, and I'd grown up feeling like I knew the guy! I can only imagine how Hamish felt to be sharing the world's most off-putting handshake with a near-drooling stranger. It was time to give up and retreat. 'I'm sorry,' I said meekly as I uncoupled from his fist. 'I'll go away now.'

Not surprisingly, Hamish and I didn't become instant friends.

There are countless phobias that haunt the corridors of the human condition. I'm intimately familiar with a couple of them: achluophobia (fear of the dark) and ophidiophobia (fear of snakes). Thankfully I was spared when it came to glosso-phobia (fear of public speaking).

One phobia we don't hear much about, however, is atychiphobia – the abnormal, unwarranted and persistent fear of failure. According to researchers at Penn State University it affects between 2 and 5 per cent of the US population. In its chronic form atychiphobia can result in difficulty breathing, an elevated heart rate, dizziness, nausea and digestive distress, and an overall feeling of dread. More universally, it leads to paralysing inaction and personal stagnation through fear of failing to achieve goals or outcomes.

While acute atychiphobia affects a mercifully small percentage of the population, a more generalised and very real fear of failure is something most of us are familiar with, in the same way many people fear spiders but not with the same debilitating terror as a chronic arachnophobe. At some point in our lives, most of us will be so hamstrung by a fear of failure that we won't take a risk that could just as easily result in success.

Take work for example. When we fear failure so much that we don't apply for a new job or put in for a promotion, we guarantee that we won't succeed. The same dynamic plays out in intimate relationships. How many people have decided not to ask someone out on a date for fear of rejection, and perhaps missed out on meeting the love of their life? Then there's the generalised fear of not measuring up to perceived standards, either set by society or ourselves. Remember, there was a time I was so fearful of failing as a primary schoolteacher – a job I already had – that my entire anus went into spasm.

Not that success in a given field is necessarily an antidote to the fear of failure. Barbra Streisand has sold 145 million albums worldwide but for twenty-seven years she didn't perform live because she was terrified of forgetting the words to her songs. 'I don't want to disappoint people,' she explained in 2018. That's the fear of not meeting standards and the fear of letting other people down rolled into a quarter-century-long battle with glossophobia.

For some, fear of failure is connected to the perfectionism we talked about in Chapters 7 and 8, but there are myriad other reasons it creeps into our psyches. Unlike irrational fears experienced by young children (and me!), such as fear of the dark, it's thought the 'rational' fear of failure is more likely to develop as we encounter opportunities where we are likely to perceive a failure, such as at school or in other organised and other measurable settings like sport.

Fear of failure is not necessarily a bad thing, though. Research has shown a moderate sense of rational fear can cause students to study harder. For example, many students complete their homework not because they enjoy it, but because they fear getting in trouble at school or disappointing their parents.

But being eager to meet certain standards is unhelpful when students become *overly* concerned about failing. When that happens people find it hard to concentrate because they're preoccupied with trying to cope with stress and anxiety associated with the activity. These young people tend to avoid challenging situations that would otherwise benefit their personal growth. Their fear can manifest as procrastination, misbehaviour and the withholding of effort – behaviours that can follow them the rest of their lives. Recognising this and overcoming it is one of the things I talk to kids about when I visit schools around the country.

EXERCISE
How to let go of fear of failure

Mid-2021 I was lucky enough to appear on broadcaster and comedian Wil Anderson's podcast *Wilosophy*. Wil concluded our interview by asking me, 'What would you do if you couldn't possibly fail?' I'm a fan of his podcast so I knew this question was coming, but despite listening to his guests fumble for an answer on multiple occasions, I'd never thought about my own response and was unprepared. Without thinking, I said, 'I'd do a show at the Melbourne International Comedy Festival.' *What?* I couldn't believe what just came out of my mouth. Or that I'd said it to one of Australia's most successful stand-up comedians!

I felt embarrassed for a while, but somehow saying this out loud got me seriously thinking about it.

1. What would failing actually look like?
2. What would happen if I did fail?

3. How would failing actually change my life?

Exploring these questions made me realise that if I didn't put on a great show, yes, it would hurt and, yes, I would most likely be very disappointed. But in time, I would turn that disappointment into a hunger to get better and learn. My failure would inevitably lead to growth. As a result of this seemingly innocuous question from Wil, my somewhat random collection of stories is now part of the 2022 Melbourne International Comedy Festival.

So if there's something that you want to try your hand at, but haven't due to the fear of failure, try working your way through those three questions.

You never know, it might just be the one thing that encourages you to take a life-changing risk.

Discussing your fear of failure can also help put it into context, in much the same way as owning our own stories, as discussed in Chapter 2, can help us understand that we all stuff up or feel embarrassment from time to time.

I'd been booked to speak to the students of Berwick Public School in outer Melbourne on the morning of my massive cafe fail with Hamish Blake and I berated myself for forty-five minutes along the entire length of the Monash Freeway. What's the matter with you? I self-heckled. You could have just said hi, thanked the man, wished him well and left him alone.

Needless to say, this sort of negative self-talk did me no favours.

As I introduced myself to the three hundred little people sitting cross-legged in the hall, I felt flat as a tack. My job was to teach them skills that would help them be more resilient in life, so I decided to harness my experience from that morning. I knew from experience that choosing honesty could be a great way to forge a connection. 'I actually feel a little bad about myself today,' I said. 'Does anyone know who Hamish Blake is?'

By the time I got to the part about putting my hands on my ribs like a chicken, the kids were rolling on the floor, shrieking with laughter. What I had considered an enormous flop looked like anything but from the kids' perspective. That story went on to have a life of its own.

During a talk to another group of kids in Clermont in central Queensland, the story brought about some unexpected growth for me – as well as serving as an ice-breaker. Towards the end of my retelling of the 'handshake from hell', a 10-year-old boy asked, 'So, you gear-sticked him?'

I didn't understand what he meant. 'Sorry mate,' I said. 'Can you repeat that?'

'You gear-sticked Hamish Blake!' he cried. 'That's what it's called when you shake like that, like grabbing the gearstick in the car.' The other kids nodded in solemn agreement. There was no laughter that day, but plenty of empathy. 'Don't worry about it,' the boy said. 'It happens to the best of us.'

And herein lies the point. This 10-year-old boy was absolutely spot on, it *does* happen to the best of us. In fact, it happens to all of us. Failure is an inevitable part of our existence. But we have to start leaning in to failure, no matter how catastrophic, and see it as an incredible opportunity for growth and improvement.

CHAPTER 10
LIFE OF RYAN

Hamish and Andy aren't the only comedians I admire. I'm also a huge fan of their friend and collaborator Ryan Shelton. In his long and varied career, Ryan has written material for Hamish and Andy's TV shows, and helped Chris Lilley write characters for the mockumentary series *We Can Be Heroes*. He's as funny in front of the camera as he is with the pen, and his segment 'Philosophisationing with Ryan Shelton' was the main reason I'd tune in to Rove McManus's show, *Rove Live*, during the early 2000s.

When that program ended in 2009 I was disappointed Ryan seemed to go a bit quiet. To my mind there was a conspicuous empty space on the national stage. Keen to consume anything he was involved with, I started following him on Instagram where he occasionally posted weird and wonderful sketches featuring his bizarre ensemble of alter egos. These never failed to put a smile on my face and I often relied on the clips to get me in the right frame of mind before a school presentation.

Fast forward to 2015 and as I entered one of my favourite cafes to do a bit of admin work, I spied Ryan sitting alone at a table, tapping away on a laptop. Not wanting to find myself in another 'gear-sticking' incident, as with Hamish Blake the previous year, I told myself not to interrupt the man. It wasn't so much that he was working – it was more that I didn't want to make a fool of myself again. I didn't want to fail.

Being such a big fan, however, and the cafe being quite small, I pulled up a chair right alongside him. Upon reflection, I literally couldn't have sat any closer without touching him. I nonchalantly flipped open my laptop and tried to read a few emails but there was no way I could focus on work when all I could think was, Holy shit! Ryan Shelton is sitting right there!

I remained awkwardly close to Ryan for half an hour

before I finally pushed through my fear of failure. Stretching my arms above my head, I casually looked over at him and acted like I'd just noticed there was someone seated next to me. 'Oh wow, Ryan Shelton!' I said, sounding as surprised as I could. 'I didn't see you there. Mate, I'm actually a big fan of your work. I love everything you do.'

'Thank you,' he said, warmly. 'That's really kind of you to say.'

Before he could turn his attention back to his laptop, I hit him with another barrage of adulation. 'You've actually been a huge help to me over the years,' I said earnestly. 'My job involves going into schools and talking to kids, and I find it impossible to do that unless I'm feeling happy.

'Sometimes when I'm sitting in my car before a talk, if I don't feel happy, I watch your Instagram videos to get myself in the best possible headspace. So, I just want to thank you for that.'

Ryan looked surprised and genuinely moved. 'Mate, that's the loveliest feedback I think I've ever heard. Thank you. What do you talk to the kids about?'

'Happiness and a bit of mental health stuff,' I said off-handedly, not wanting to change the topic from Ryan.

'And where do you do—' he continued before I cut him off.

'Can I get a photo? My girlfriend loves you!' I added, which was true, but I wasn't getting the picture for Penny.

Ryan obligingly posed for a selfie. I thanked him then we said our goodbyes, as if one of us was about to pack up and leave. It quickly became obvious that neither of us was going anywhere. We stiffly returned to our laptops and worked silently, side by side, for the next thirty minutes.

Later that day I posted the photo on Instagram and tagged Ryan in the desperate hope he might 'like' it. Later I was thrilled to see he'd given the photo the thumbs up. 'Well, that was one of the best days of my life,' I said to Penny before turning in that night. I was over the moon.

Four years later, in early 2019, I was cleaning up after dinner when my phone pinged with a notification of an Instagram message. 'Hi mate, hope you're well,' it read. 'I was wondering if we could catch up? Cheers, Ryan.'

I had to read it twice then check again to make sure it was really a message from the great philosophisationer. 'Holy shit, Ryan bloody Shelton just messaged me,' I gasped as I spun around to face Penny.

'Okay, just play it cool,' she said. 'Don't write back straight away. Give it some time.'

Too late. I was already typing a reply. 'Yes! Definitely! When? Tomorrow?'

We arranged to catch up at Archie's, the same cafe where we'd met four years prior. True to form, fear of failure caused me to obsess over how to present myself at what promised to be, in my mind, a historic summit.

Should I go early and already be sitting down when Ryan arrives? Or will that make me look too desperate? I wondered. Fashionably late could look cool. But what if *he's* early and I'm late? I might seem unreliable or uninterested.

As it turned out we arrived at exactly the same time. 'Hey mate!' I said, trying to sound as relaxed as I could. I still had no idea why Ryan wanted to meet with me. We exchanged pleasantries for all of two minutes before he came straight to the point. 'I feel really lost at the moment,' he said.

It was the last thing I'd been expecting to hear.

'I was having dinner with my girlfriend Jam the other night,' he explained, 'and I told her that for my entire life all I've ever wanted was my own TV show.'

Here was me, a fan, thinking Ryan Shelton had already achieved huge success in television – more than most people could dream of. He was a great writer and a brilliant performer with plenty of hits under his belt. If he wasn't a success, then who was?

'Then I realised having my own show wouldn't be enough for me to feel happy,' he continued. 'To be happy, I'd need to be winning awards for the best show on television. I'd need to be heralded as the funniest person in Australia.'

I could feel there was a point coming so I didn't interrupt.

'So, I was sitting there, explaining this to Jam when I realised something: even if I had my own show and it was the funniest, most awarded comedy of all time, I don't think that would be enough to make me happy. And . . . I've been feeling lost ever since.'

It was a lot to take in from a bloke I hardly knew. It had to be one of the most vulnerable conversations I'd ever had from a standing start. It bonded us almost immediately. It was clear Ryan was looking for some guidance outside of what his friends and family could offer. I didn't presume to have the answers to his problems so I mostly just listened.

After a few coffees, we said our farewells (with a normal handshake) and promised to catch up again soon. Back at home I fell over myself telling Penny all about the meeting. 'When do you think is too soon to message him?' I said.

'Why do you need to message him?' she asked.

'Oh, you know, just to say thanks and how I really enjoyed catching up.'

'It sounds like a first date!' she said with a chuckle.

I was soon meeting Ryan for coffee once a week. We'd talk about all types of issues in our lives: stuff men don't ordinarily open up about with other men. Over lunch one day, Ryan shared something he'd been struggling with regarding his best mate – one Hamish Blake. They'd been close since their teenage years and had worked together writing and producing comedy for a long time. But because of a story Ryan had been telling himself, he found it increasingly hard to celebrate the rise and rise of his friend's star.

Along with Hamish, Andy Lee and Tim Bartley, Ryan was a founding member of the TV production company Radio Karate. But instead of being proud of this fact, Ryan had begun telling himself the toxic story that the only reason the other three involved him was because they felt sorry for him. Furthermore, he'd started whispering to himself that the sole reason he got any opportunities outside of Hamish and Andy was because of his friendship with them.

'Have you told Hamish that?' I asked.

Ryan shook his head.

'You need to tell him,' I said, 'because I reckon you're telling yourself a very unkind story; a very unfair version of events. If you shared it with Hamish I think you'd find he's got a very different take on things.'

As I spoke Ryan's eyes welled up. 'You're right,' he said.

Getting to know Ryan underscored for me that no matter how great someone's life appears to be from afar, no one is living the perfect existence. I had always looked up to the likes of Ryan and Hamish, and imagined they were constantly creatively fulfilled, universally admired and thriving financially. It was humbling and almost reassuring to discover Ryan struggled with shame, expectation and the fear of failure, just like everybody else.

It was in that realisation that the seed for the podcast that eventually became *The Imperfects* was planted. For years people had told me I should do a podcast on resilience but my response was always the same: 'Only once I have an idea that's unique and that will help people.'

That night I texted Ryan at 11.30. 'I've had an idea for a podcast,' I said. 'Based on our chat today about you and Hamish, I feel it'd be great to get well-known, successful people to share their struggles, from the heart. Maybe we could do it together?'

'Sounds amazing,' Ryan said, 'but you don't need me. I'm happy to help out in the background.' It took me (and Ryan's girlfriend Jam) about six months to convince him he should co-host the podcast. It took another six months before we released our first episode.

To cut a long (development) story short, I got a small

glimpse into why Radio Karate, and indeed Hamish and Andy, have been so wildly successful. Ryan introduced me to a level of professionalism, planning, consideration and patience that I had not known before. Had it been up to me, I would have released episode one of *The Imperfects* the day after Ryan agreed to take part.

The other pivotal moment came when we approached my brother Josh – a gifted director and storyteller – to help us produce it. Working on *The Imperfects* with those two blokes is one of the greatest joys I have ever known. Ryan's humour and quick wit make the sometimes heavy topics we discuss accessible to all. The time, effort and skill that Josh puts into crafting each episode is an art form in itself. I am very fortunate to have a front row seat to watch them do what they do best.

A NOTE ON FRIENDSHIP

While *The Imperfects* is essentially about our guests, one keen listener emailed me with an unexpected observation:

I love the stories of your guests but I'm more intrigued by the dynamics of your friendships and the way in which

the relationship between the three of you is developing.
It's great modelling of what a real and healthy friendship
should look like.

It was an astute take on a topic I'd been pondering for a while. What are the ingredients of a healthy friendship? Since starting the podcast, I'd grown quite close to Ryan. I'd also noticed a powerful shift in my relationship with my brother Josh. Although Josh and I often texted 'I love you' to each other, we hadn't actually said it out loud for a very long time. Thanks to the podcast, I've been able to say it to his face.

While exploring the subject of friendship, I stumbled across a fascinating piece of research that showed the proof of a good friendship is found not so much in how people react if you need help or when the chips are down – but in how they respond to your good news.

University of California psychology professor Shelly Gable looked deeply into the dynamics of friendship and identified four possible reactions to the sharing of good news.[1]

- Active-constructive: Characterised by enthusiasm, genuine interest and support. Such a friend might say, 'You got a promotion? That's amazing! I'm thrilled for you. You have worked so hard for that. Tell me exactly how it happened.'

- Passive-constructive: This person *appears* to be positive but only offers a muted response and doesn't want any more details beyond what you have provided. They might offer a 'Well done' or a 'That's great' with no sign of enthusiasm or interest.
- Active-destructive: The belittling or reinterpretation of your good news, with a focus on negatives. This person might say, 'You got a promotion? I hope you're ready to work one hundred hours a week and never see your family.' These people will often make it about them. 'I haven't had a promotion in ages' might be another response.
- Passive-destructive: This person barely acknowledges your good news, or changes the subject entirely. 'You got a promotion? You should get a load of the fishing trip I've got planned next week!'

We all know people who give those responses, the good and the bad. Penny and I have a couple of friends who are textbook 'passive-destructive'.

When we announced Penny was pregnant: 'Oh, we won't be having kids for ages, we just don't want the stress and hassle of it all.'

When we bought a house: 'Yeah, we'll probably buy a house soon but not in that suburb, that's for sure.'

We still like these people, but our relationships with them are not among the deepest in our lives.

The more I thought about it, I realised the strongest bonds are with those I call when I have good news. I've known Ryan for a fraction of my life, and Josh for thirty-four years, yet they are both my go-to people when I've got good news. I put it down to shared vulnerability.

When I told Ryan The Resilience Project had been asked to partner with Steve's supermarket chain, his response was a masterclass in connection and empathy – what Professor Shelly Gable would call 'active-constructive'.

'Wow-eee!' he beamed down the phone. 'Tell me everything! How did this happen? Who gave you the good news? How did you feel?'

As tight as we had become, Ryan was still yet to act on my advice to talk to Hamish Blake about his feelings. While The Imperfects kept him busy, Ryan had so much more to offer the world but his quest for meaning and purpose proved elusive. 'If I'm not trying to have my own TV show, and be the funniest man alive, then what's the purpose of doing all this?' he said one day.

I'd noticed he'd stopped posting videos to Instagram. When he mentioned the word 'purpose' it started to make sense. I didn't know how to help him find his purpose but I knew someone who could. In 2019 I introduced Ryan to Ben Crowe. Ben led him to the realisation that his purpose in life wasn't to be the funniest man in Australia or have the highest-rating, most-awarded show on TV – it was simply to spread joy using humour and creativity.

Soon after Ryan articulated this purpose he went live on Instagram with a fifteen-minute clip of him dancing around his house in a wig – his first output on the platform for eighteen months. It was one of the most extraordinary performances I have ever seen. It made me cry with laughter. When it ended, he signed off with the words, 'Anyway, I'm back.'

And he's been back ever since. The crystallisation of Ryan's purpose uncorked his creativity in the most wonderful way. A chorus line of ridiculous new characters was dreamt up, classic Ryan Shelton skits were penned and hilarious videos were filmed and uploaded to his website ryyyyyyyyyyyyan.com (the eleven y's serve to remind fans a new clip is uploaded on the eleventh of every month). All this activity is dedicated solely to spreading joy using creativity and humour.

As a mate, I feel privileged to have played a very small role in the re-emergence of Ryan Shelton, the comedian, but as a fan I am over the moon. I now get to see new material from my favourite performer every single month. It brings me so much joy, which is the very fulfilment of his purpose.

It's quite likely Ryan would have figured this out for himself but none of it would have panned out the way it has had I yielded to the fear of failure and left him in peace with his laptop at Archie's cafe all those years ago. Not the meeting with Ben about purpose, not the inception of *The Imperfects* podcast and certainly not our friendship.

It took him a year but Ryan eventually told Hamish Blake what had been troubling him. Hamish responded the way I expected he would: by reality-checking Ryan's shame in real time.

In the space of a few minutes, years of poisonous thought vanished under the glaring sunlight of honesty and vulnerability. Ryan says he hasn't looked back since.

One final shame story

In 2019 Ryan came to see me speak publicly for the first time. As I was getting ready to go onstage at the Melbourne Convention Centre, one of the staff stuck her head in the green room and said, 'Can you please tell the Hamish Blake story tonight? It's my all-time favourite.'

For years I had been telling the Hamish Blake gear-sticking story all around the country, to hundreds and thousands of people. Evidently I'd told it the last time I appeared at the Convention Centre.

'I can't tell it tonight,' I sheepishly replied to the young usher. 'I'm really sorry. It's just . . . I just can't.'

'How come?' she asked.

I get extremely chatty when I'm nervous so I took her through it in detail, beginning with the day I met Ryan for the first time.

'. . . And so,' I concluded after five minutes, 'Ryan's in the audience tonight and I'm worried that if he hears that story he'll think the only reason we're friends is because I wanted to meet his mate Hamish Blake, which is absurd, but I don't want to run the risk of triggering him.'

'You need to tell Ryan this,' she said.

The teenage usher had given me a serving of my own shame medicine, and she was absolutely spot on. I eventually worked up the courage to have that conversation with Ryan. I even found footage of me telling the story and shared it with him. 'Just so you know, I am friends with you because of who you are,' I said nervously. 'You do know that, don't you?'

'Of course I do!' he said with an expression that suggested it was the most obvious thing I'd ever said. In a heartbeat he'd moved on to another topic and just like that, my worry was gone.

SOCIAL MEDIA

CHAPTER 11

GOING WITH THE FLOW

Saturday 25 November 2006 signalled the end of an era for the van Cuylenburg family. Georgia and I had grown up and flown the coop, and Mum and Dad had put the family home on the market. I understood, but I was devastated. To me the place wasn't just a building, it was a grand old ship – a majestic galleon that had carried us through the tempest and tranquillity of our formative years. I hated to think someone else would soon be taking it over, but I knew Mum and Dad needed to downsize and I just hoped they'd get a good price.

The auction was due to start at 12.30 pm. Since it was summertime I was at cricket, naturally. The game started at 11 am but all I could think about on the way to the ground was the impending loss of the family home. I made a mental note to phone Mum and Dad to wish them luck before bidding began. During a drinks break I jogged off the pitch and fished my phone out of my bag. Just as I was about to dial Dad's number I realised it was 4.25 pm.

'What the hell just happened?' I said out loud. Five hours of my life had seemingly disappeared. I could have sworn we'd been playing for under an hour.

I needn't have worried about the auction, though: the house was sold and Mum and Dad were really happy. What will the new owners do with the place? I wondered. Will they keep the basketball ring? Surely! It's got a brand new net. And what about the cricket pitch? If they have an ounce of common sense they'll recognise a quality batting surface that has been meticulously curated and cared for for more than twenty years. You can't just do away with something as beautiful as that.

Two weeks after Mum and Dad handed over the keys I did a sentimental drive-by. As I cruised along my life's most travelled street I felt a sharp pain in my heart.

The entire property had been levelled.

Trees, house, gardens and lawns – all bulldozed flat.

I felt like Princess Leia in *Star Wars* when her home planet of Alderaan is destroyed by the Death Star.

The day of the auction wasn't the first time I'd lost track of time while playing cricket. A while after I had retired from my twenty-one years of playing Victorian Premier Cricket, I learnt the mysterious time warp has a name: 'transient hypofrontality'. It describes a temporary reduction of activity – under certain conditions – in the prefrontal cortex of the brain. This is the part where decision-making and systematic thinking occurs. When transient hypofrontality occurs, the highly focused 'thinking part' of our brain takes a back seat, allowing other brain functions to become more dominant. This fascinating phenomenon is more commonly known as 'flow state' or just 'flow'.

According to bestselling US journalist and executive director to the Flow Research Collective, Steven Kolter, 'flow' describes times of total absorption when we are so focused on what we are doing that everything else seems to disappear.

'Our sense of self, our sense of self-consciousness, they vanish,' Kolter explains. 'Time dilates which means sometimes it slows down. You get that freeze frame effect familiar to any of you who have seen *The Matrix* or been in a car crash. Sometimes it speeds up and five hours will pass by in like five minutes. And throughout, all aspects of performance, mental and physical, go through the roof.'[1]

I'm firmly in the 'time speeds up' column. I missed a lot of things about cricket when I retired: the competition, the camaraderie, the physical test, and bowling long spells in the hot sun. It wasn't until I read Kolter's research into flow – and how it captured my experience with cricket to a tee – that I realised what I missed most about cricket was the access it gave me to transient hypofrontality. I love being in flow.

When I resumed my athletics career in 2019, I was delighted to rediscover that feeling. Training at the track usually accounts for two hours but, without fail, those 120 minutes feel like they pass in around ten. I could live without the time warp to be honest (so could Penny, since I'm always running late) but the thing I love about flow is that my inner critic – the sneering voice that resides in my prefrontal cortex – is silenced for a while. There's not a syllable of negative self-talk when I'm running. There wasn't when I played cricket, either.

Aside from the resultant boost to my self-esteem, when I'm in flow, I'm also able to conjure ambitious ideas and plans for The Resilience Project, and imagine wonderful things we could do as a family. I'm filled with a sense of excitement about the future.

Running, and the flow state it delivers, was a huge mental lifeline for me during the rolling COVID-19 lockdowns of 2020–21. About two months into Melbourne's marathon 125-day lockdown in 2020, I developed an intense pain in the top of my leg. A telehealth session with my physio revealed I had proximal hamstring tendinopathy.

'How long is this going to stop me running?' I asked.

'One hundred days,' he replied. 'That's what it takes for tendons to heal properly.'

Maybe he thought 'one hundred days' sounded less daunting than 'three-and-a-bit months' but it didn't. And there was more bad news. 'You can't sit down for those hundred days, either.'

If I wanted my leg to get better I would have to semi-sit, semi-kneel in one of those weird ergonomic chairs Darryl Kerrigan made famous in *The Castle*. My physio sent me a giant elastic band and a schedule of monotonous hamstring exercises. 'Once a week you can go for a light three-kilometre jog,' he added. 'But that's it.'

When the call was over I flopped onto the bed, totally dejected. Bloody hell, I'm in trouble here, I thought. That same day, 725 coronavirus cases were recorded in Victoria.

We were forbidden from leaving home unless it was to shop or exercise, we couldn't travel more than five kilometres from home and the kids weren't sleeping well. Now my mental escape hatch into the river of flow had been slammed shut, too. In the lowest year of my life, I had reached the nadir.

It was a cold and miserable Melbourne winter, and I had already been cut off from my other form of mental happiness – engaging with people at public talks around the country. This was another part of life where I experienced flow. It doesn't happen every time I get on stage – in fact, it's rare. But when it does happen, it's the most extraordinary out-of-body experience. Far more than anything I have experienced in cricket or running. It's like I exit my body, float to the side the of stage and watch myself perform. It's the best feeling in the world.

I was wallowing in my misery one particularly freezing day when an email from the not-for-profit group Down Syndrome Victoria appeared in my inbox.

It explained how the organisation ran a group called Club 21, comprising adults from around Melbourne who got together at a social event every week. Lockdown had put an end to that. 'They haven't caught up now in three months,' the message read. 'They're really struggling without face-to-face contact.'

My dismay over the fact I couldn't go for a run suddenly felt somewhat overblown. Down Syndrome Victoria wanted to know if I could organise some resilience journals for the members of Club 21. I looked at my family, happily tussling over some soft toys on the floor of the lounge room, and realised how lucky I was to have the people I love most just an arm's length away.

'I'd love to help you,' I replied. 'I can organise some journals but I'm happy to volunteer my time, too. Why don't I run a Zoom session for them?'

It turned out Club 21 had already adapted to Zoom during lockdown and met online once a fortnight. We decided I'd drop in to their next meeting which, as luck would have it, was in a few days' time. I was told the catch-up lasted an hour so I spent half a day figuring out what I'd talk to them about, organising slides and videos, and preparing some activities around gratitude, empathy and mindfulness.

When the day came I logged in to the Zoom call fifteen minutes before the session was due to start at 3 pm, just to make sure I had all my ducks in a row before the Club 21 members logged on. As soon as I opened the link to the call I was surprised to see forty faces beaming back at me. Apparently being early and having your ducks in a row was a Club 21 trait, too.

Before I could open my mouth one of the members unmuted himself. 'Hello Hugh, my name is Dean. I'd like to officially welcome you to Club 21. We're so excited to have you and we can't wait for your session.'

I was trying to get my head around the fact we were starting fifteen minutes early, since I'd only prepared material for an hour session, when another bloke unmuted himself. 'I would also like to officially welcome you to Club 21,' he said.

'Hi Hugh, my name is Sarah,' said the next person to unmute. 'I want to welcome you to Club 21, too. Thanks for joining us.'

For the next twenty-five minutes or so I was showered with the warmest, most heartfelt greetings as each member introduced themselves and made me feel welcome. By the time I'd met them all individually we were running well behind schedule. I worried whether I'd be able to squeeze the material I'd prepared into less than an hour.

'Excuse me, Hugh,' another young woman piped up, 'I'm just letting you know I have to leave at three-thirty today, so don't be surprised when I disappear.'

'Sure, that's fine,' I said. 'Do you have somewhere else you need to be?'

'No,' she said, 'I just feel like relaxing at three-thirty.'

'Right,' I said, trying hard not to laugh. 'If you disappear I'll understand.'

We'd only just begun but I was already in love with the members of Club 21. I decided to forget about the presentation I'd prepared and just chat instead. I was totally absorbed in getting to know them which, after all, is what being in a club is all about. I told them about myself and they took turns telling me about their hobbies and interests. A guy named Steve went first.

'I like women,' he said.

'Oh,' I said and nodded, smiling. 'Do you now?'

'Yes I do. And swimming,' he added. 'Women and swimming.'

Another bloke had an actual microphone on a lead connected to his computer, and he held it like he was Freddie Mercury.

'What are you into, mate?' I asked.

'I like to drink,' he said matter-of-factly.

'Oh right, so what? Milkshakes? Smoothies? Juice?'

'Nup!' he said, bending forward and almost swallowing the mic. 'I like booze. Straight booze.'

The Club 21 crew were some of the best people I had met in a very long time. No wonder they missed connecting with each other face to face. While they made me laugh often, they were also masters of vulnerability. They never held back when expressing how much they missed and loved each other.

Although we'd abandoned a structured session, I suggested we talk a bit about our loved ones – after all, the session was supposed to be about connecting. I went first and reeled off stock-standard, run-of-the-mill information about my family: names, ages, occupations and interests. I then sat back and was given a masterclass in how to talk about the people you love most in the world.

One of the first to speak was a chatty girl with thick brown hair. 'Sometimes, after a long day at work, I'm too tired to tell my brother how much I love him so I just give him a big cuddle instead,' she said. 'He knows from my cuddle how much I love him.'

'I'd also like to cuddle your brother,' said another from the group, followed by everyone else adding how they, too, would enjoy cuddling this girl's brother. She responded to all of them individually. 'You would really like cuddling him.'

One of the younger guys told us he loved the way his mum smelt because it made him feel instantly happy. I knew exactly what he meant. 'But not Dad,' he said firmly. 'That's a totally different story.'

This was met with unanimous agreement. So much for my role as guest facilitator: they didn't need me. So I sat back, smiling with tears in my eyes. I had only spent a short time in their company, but I felt so engaged and stimulated, a very strong bond took hold. All too soon the session's convenor, the wonderful Alison from Down Syndrome Victoria, moved to wrap things up.

'Okay guys, we're probably going to have to let Hugh go now,' she said.

'No, we're good!' I quickly replied. 'I'm really happy to hang out here until four o'clock.'

When Alison pointed out it was well past 4 pm I was stunned. We'd been talking nearly an hour and a half but I could have sworn it was no more than twenty minutes. Once again I'd stumbled into an activity where I experienced transient hypofrontality. I knew then it wouldn't be my last session with Club 21.

The neuroscience behind flow is fascinating. When the prefrontal cortex gets a rest, other impulses that aren't governed by critical thinking, like creativity or risk-taking, get a chance to take over. In my case I've noticed bold, positive thoughts get an airing while I'm running, speaking to an audience and, evidently, when working with the men and women of Club 21.

Transient hypofrontality goes by many names. In the NBA, basketballers refer to it as 'being unconscious'. Other elite sportspeople say it puts them 'in the zone' while jazz musicians refer to it as being 'in the pocket'.

Professor Mihaly Csikszentmihalyi, a Hungarian–American psychologist, was the first person to recognise this heightened mental state and give it a name. Professor Csikszentmihalyi describes flow as providing 'a sense of discovery, a creative feeling of transporting a person into a higher reality'.[2]

Professor of cognitive neuroscience Arne Dietrich, of the American University of Beirut, has also studied flow and points to its key characteristics as being:

- Distractions being eliminated from awareness
- Time losing its meaning
- The ego taking a leave of absence.[3]

What all of this describes is the condition most of us have experienced at one point or another – when we are simply functioning at our best. Professor Csikszentmihalyi says flow is achieved when an activity challenges us enough to bring heightened focus onto the action, but not so much that it overwhelms our consciousness. While we need mastery of the skills involved, we still need to be pushed to drive those abilities further. In that balance between boredom and anxiety we arrive at what scientists call the 'flow channel'.

Flow is also the only time the human brain releases the four 'feel good' hormones – oxytocin, dopamine, serotonin and endorphins – *simultaneously*. Professor Csikszentmihalyi says this delivers four major benefits:

- Heightened concentration
- Clarity of thought
- No obstacles to our thought processes
- Positive feelings.

Now, before you move on to the next page, ask yourself this: How often have you felt in flow while staring at the screen of your smartphone?

CHAPTER 12

A FILE CALLED REGRET, TAKE TWO

In my first book, *The Resilience Project*, I wrote about why we need to leave our phones at home, how we should rearrange our home screens in order to dull the appeal of technology, and how we ought to thwart Silicon Valley's army of addiction engineers by switching off our notifications. I lived by that advice and led by example, and those measures served me well. Right up until there was a global pandemic, that is. When COVID-19 arrived and the lockdowns began, I went straight to my phone in order to connect – just like everyone else. And almost overnight I found myself on a slippery slope.

One beautiful spring afternoon in between lockdowns I headed to the local playground with Mum and my son Benji. After cheering Benji on as he conquered the slide for the fifteenth time, I started to feel distracted. Bored, if I'm honest. Before I knew it I was looking at the little screen in my palm, searching for distraction, validation . . . *something*. Sometimes we don't even know why we look at the bloody things.

I felt Mum's eyes upon me even before I glanced up. She had a very disapproving expression on her face.

'I'm just waiting on an important email,' I lied. 'I just need to check it for a minute.'

This rubbish was met with a look of disappointment. Mum held my gaze for a second or two before shaking her head and turning her attention to Benji.

'Mum, it's a really important email,' I doubled down, kidding myself as much as I was trying to kid her. 'It means a lot.'

'You know what, Hugh?' she said. 'It's not Benji I feel sorry for right now. It's you.' Mum gestured around the playground: the sweep of her hand taking in multiple mums and dads who were mesmerised, not by their children, but by the little electronic devices in their hands. 'It's your whole generation of parents I feel sorry for, actually,' she added.

I have countless wonderful memories of being at the park

as a kid with Mum. Carefree days before mobile phones. But Benji? I imagine a lot of his memories from the park involve me hunched over my device like some sort of digital junky.

'When I was your age and you were Benji's age, I saw everything you saw,' Mum went on. 'I heard everything you heard and I smelt everything you smelt. I was there with you every single step. I experienced the world as you did.'

She really had my attention now. I pushed my phone guiltily back into my jeans pocket.

'And because of that, as an older person, I'm filled with the most incredible memories and emotions,' she said. 'I can't walk past a jasmine bush without getting emotional because when you were a boy there was nothing you loved more than the smell of those flowers.'

Mum tilted her face to the vivid blue sky. 'On days like this, when there wasn't a single cloud, you used to get so excited. And now, every time the weather's beautiful, I'm reminded of the joy you found in the simple things in life. I'm sorry you won't have that as you and Benji grow older. Your generation isn't properly here with your kids.'

Mum has always been the exemplar of how I want to conduct myself, particularly when it comes to emotions and personal connections. Our 'emotional literacy' – knowing how to put our feelings into words and communicate them clearly to ourselves and others – is forged in the home. I was lucky Mum had an incredible instinct for the importance of emotional literacy.

She was forever asking me how I felt and telling me what emotions she was experiencing, too. One of her earliest lessons in emotional literacy came about as the result of my first-ever playdate. In kindergarten I was in awe of a boy in my class named Andy Moss. 'Mossy' had to be the coolest kid in kinder and when I was invited to his house after school I thought all my Christmases had come at once.

As soon as I turned up with Mum, Mossy and I ran off to play in his room while Mum sat down in the kitchen for a cup of tea with Mrs Moss.

'Do you want to look inside my cupboard?' Mossy asked me as we entered his bedroom.

'Oh yeah, I'd love to,' I squeaked excitedly.

Mossy opened his cupboard door, ushered me inside and closed it behind me. 'You stay in there and I'll play with my toys,' his muffled voice instructed from the outside world, as if it were a perfectly normal thing to do on a playdate.

I was too shy to argue with Mossy's unorthodox approach

to entertaining so I sat in the pitch-dark cupboard for an hour until it was time to go. I was very quiet in the car on the way home.

'Are you okay?' Mum asked.

I hummed a little non-answer. I didn't really know what to say.

'How are you feeling, darling?' she pressed.

'I feel sad,' I finally admitted.

'Why do you feel sad?'

When I told her about sitting in Mossy's cupboard, she looked at me empathetically and said, 'I'd feel sad if someone locked me in a cupboard for an hour, too. I think that's exactly how you should feel if someone does that to you.'

For the rest of the ride home we talked about sadness: the other times I'd felt sad in my life, the times Mum had felt sad, what we did when the feeling took hold and how, in time, the sadness passed and we learnt something from it (in the latest instance, not to sit in a cupboard just because someone tells you to).

By the time we got home, thanks to Mum, I'd identified my emotion, had that emotion validated and then work-shopped possible solutions.

According to Dr Billy Garvey, a paediatrician at the Royal Children's Hospital in Melbourne, there are three things we need to do when a child (or adult, for that matter) opens up about something they're struggling with:

- Help them articulate the emotion they are feeling.
- Validate the emotion.
- Help them solve the issue.

'As parents, we are way too keen to skip the first couple of steps and just solve the problem,' Dr Garvey says. This doesn't apply just to our children. When I was burnt out and unable to get out of bed a couple of years ago, I called a few people to tell them how I was going. Just wanting to be caring and help, they all tried to solve the problem that very instant. I remember feeling no better. In fact, I felt frustrated and anxious. Not surprisingly, when I told Mum, I instantly felt a bit better. Just as she'd done following the urine-soaked show-and-tell calamity, and the great Mossy lock-in, she helped me label the emotion and then validate it. 'I totally understand why you feel that way, darling, I would feel exactly the same way.'

As I write this I am filled with a deep sense of gratitude for Mum. She has always been instinctively brilliant with scenarios like this. You can pay thousands of dollars to attend parenting courses to learn about this very process. I was so lucky, I had a front row seat every single time I went to Mum with an issue. I *still* have a front row seat. I marvel at the way she navigates life's ups and downs with my kids now. I have always felt blessed to be in touch with my emotions. It wasn't by chance, though. It was because of Mum.

As I stood in the park pretending to check emails while my son played, Mum's words hit me straight between the eyes. I knew *exactly* what she was talking about and I knew she was right. In fact, I'd been preaching the same thing around the country for years. But there I was, as guilty as the next parent of being at the park with my kid – but a thousand miles away at the same time.

The pandemic has changed us in ways that won't be properly understood for decades. It is already clear, however, that community lockdown orders supercharged the connectivity that social media offers, but opened a can of worms along the way.

Naturally, we turned to social media platforms in an attempt to fill the void and have our psychological needs met. In doing so we have spent months embedding bad habits and exposing ourselves to the tech companies' full range of dirty tricks and mind games. These strategies are really simple: they're *designed* to keep us endlessly jabbing our fingers at little computers.

Research cited by *The Age* in 2019 showed Australians spent on average more than forty-six hours a week peering at their screens (and this was before COVID and lockdowns). Not only that, we checked our smartphones around eighty-five times a day.[1] Hey, we even have a new phobia to add to the list! Nomophobia: the fear of being without a smartphone.

While online learning and Zoom lessons have been a necessary stopgap after schools were shuttered by the virus, a whole generation of kids from kindergarten to Year 12 has been given unprecedented – and practically continuous – access to devices and social media platforms they didn't have before. Children's screen time skyrocketed during the pandemic, alarming parents and scientists alike.

'There will be a period of epic withdrawal,' says Keith Humphreys, a professor of psychology at Stanford University. An addiction expert who served as an adviser to President Barack Obama, Professor Humphreys believes the 'great digital detox' of the young will require them to 'sustain attention in normal interactions without getting a reward hit every few seconds'.[2]

In some ways my advice about dealing with social media and screen addiction was swamped by COVID-19's tsunami of rapid social change. While the measures I suggested still hold true, I have come to realise – with a little help from my loving mum – that we'll need to work much harder in the wake of the pandemic to let go of our addiction to social media and devices.

The stakes are high. According to Educare, a company dedicated to the welfare of young people in regional New South Wales, excessive use of technology leads to anxiety and depression, a reduction in self-esteem and life satisfaction, and lower emotional stability. Kids who develop addictions to social media and gaming are more likely to be sleep-deprived and prone to feelings of tension.

Our own research at The Resilience Project has given us startling insight into the problem. Students at every school we work with undertake the 'Resilient Youth Survey'. This helps us assess and profile the school's wellbeing. Of the 320,000 school students who took part in the program in 2020, 39 per cent of secondary students told us they text message their friends between 10 pm and 6 am. Even more alarming, 18 per cent of primary students admitted to the same behaviour.

In a world where a staggering 1.38 billion smartphones were sold in 2020 alone,[3] how do we begin to find ways of helping the young – and the old – withdraw from a planet-wide chirping, beeping, vibrating, pixilated opioid?

I think part of the answer can be found in flow.

Over the past couple of years we've spent Christmas holidays on Victoria's Surf Coast, along with thousands of other families on leave from the rat race. Nearly every parent I've chatted to as our kids played on the sand or swam in the sea has remarked on how their children seem to really come alive at that time of year.

'They're in the surf for three hours, then we'll have lunch together, we chat together,' one dad gushed to me as we watched the local nippers go through their paces. 'Then they're back out at the beach or at a park in the afternoon. They don't want their phone, they have no desire to look at a screen or play a computer game. At the end of the day they're exhausted but they're exhilarated.'

It's a common story told time and again on the fine sands at Fairhaven. I believe the common denominator is that those kids are in flow. The benefits almost go without saying: negative self-talk is banished when the prefrontal cortex is disengaged and kids experience a healthy self-esteem boost thanks to the experiences they're having. They don't need to crowdsource self-esteem from social media – they're getting it from flow.

So how do we get more flow and less screen time in our lives? The advice about phones from my last book still stands. We need to:

- Delete social media apps such as Facebook and Instagram from our phones. If we want to use them we can fire up our laptop.
- Turn off all notifications – they only exist to encourage us to use an app on our phone.
- Remove all addictive apps from our home screens.
- If it's possible, leave our phones at home when we go out.

IDENTIFYING YOUR FLOW ACTIVITY

As for upping our access to transient hypofrontality, by now you're probably thinking about what your flow state activity might be. If you have an activity in mind, answer these five questions. If you answer 'yes' to all five, chances are you've identified your flow activity.

1. Do you care about the activity?
2. Is the activity not too easy but not too difficult?
3. Are you naturally good at the activity?
4. When you're doing the activity are you focused on

the journey (as opposed to the destination)? For example, if it's rock-climbing, are you thinking about the climb or the view from the top?

5. Do you lose track of time when you're doing the activity?

We can ask our kids the same questions but more often than not it's obvious when children are in flow: they're positive, they're focused and they're happy.

Getting into flow became an essential escape for me in 2021 as Melbourne's lockdowns stretched beyond the 200-day mark, but it was sometimes elusive. Trying to write this book while at home with two young kids was often a battle. The athletics track was my portal to the world of flow but I didn't always automatically click into transient hypofrontality. It was hard work. Over time, though, I found ways to align my mind with the 'flow channel':

- Create a preparation ritual: My pre-run routine has almost become an obsession. Fill two bottles of water, prepare protein drink, pack bag with headphones, foam roller, massage ball and two pairs of spikes. At the track I listen to the exact same playlist as I do the exact same warm-up that takes precisely forty minutes. By following this routine I never feel under pressure to quickly get into flow. I usually slip into flow halfway through the warm-up.

- Identify your peak creative and productive times: For me it's around 9.30 am (having had coffee). If you are able to get into your flow activity at your optimal time, your brain has a much better shot at slipping into transient hypofrontality.
- Eliminate distractions: Obviously the phone has to go. If I have mine with me, I leave it in the car when I'm running. I had to work out how to get my playlist onto my watch but once I did it was a game changer. Smartphones are kryptonite to flow state.

Running and my sessions with Club 21 got me through the hell of 2020. Both brought me immeasurable joy and satisfaction, no matter what was happening in the world around me. I also noticed on the days I ran or worked with Club 21 I had absolutely no desire to be on social media. Much like the kids on the beach at Fairhaven, I was fulfilled. I was in flow.

To explore this further I started journalling the emotions I felt during and directly after my flow activities. The pages quickly filled with positive words. When I reviewed it a few weeks later, I noticed three words in particular came up time and time again: 'love', 'belonging' and 'validated'.

This was a watershed moment in my fight against resurgent, COVID-19-inspired screen addiction. We all have a psychological need for love, a need for belonging and a need to feel validated. As I wrote in my first book, social media is designed to make us *think* we are getting our psychological needs met. Want to feel loved? Post a picture of yourself and wait for people to hit the love heart button. Want to feel like you belong? There are countless groups you can join. Want to be validated? Tell everyone on Facebook about your graduation, new outfit or promotion and watch the little white and blue thumbs pour in.

It's seemingly all within reach, all the time, but here's the thing – *none of it* truly fulfils our psychological needs.

After a particularly gruelling session on the track early in 2021, I found myself lying on my back unable to move, staring up at the sky and gasping for air. I suddenly became overwhelmed by the strongest feelings of love: love for the people in my life, love for myself, love for the incredible gift of just being alive.

As I stood up and staggered towards my bag, I felt a

strong sense of belonging to the running community – all of those other maniacs recklessly flying around the track that day. Above all else I felt validated, like I was good at something. Not because I had shared my achievement on Instagram, but because I *knew* what I had just accomplished was the result of skill and hard work.

There's an argument to be made that finding flow becomes harder the older we get. The time we can devote to activities where we experience transient hypofrontality gets squeezed by all the commitments that crowd the average adult life, especially when you have children.

The things we do to find flow – be it golf, tennis, playing music, surfing or gardening – seem to be the first things sacrificed on the altar of pressing demands and parental duties. Indulging in flow-friendly activities can come off as selfish. I think that's wrong. If you know what activities open you up to flow, then you should try as hard as you can to incorporate them into your life. Find a place where you can schedule them in and stick to the routine. Not only will you experience the benefits of flow, there's a very good chance you'll experience feelings of love, validation and belonging, too. If you're anything like me, your cravings to pick up your phone and scroll mindlessly will also sharply diminish.

■

I caught up with Club 21 on Zoom every second week throughout 2020. I never had to plan anything, I just logged in to the session and joined the conversation with my new mates. We had the most beautiful chats about the mad planet we live on, the crazy things that happen here and the foibles of the humans who crawl all over it. Without fail, I found myself in flow in those sessions but it was even better than the transient hypofrontality I experienced when running. Why? Well, I think it was because I was engaged with other people at the same time.

I learnt a lot from Club 21 and developed some great ideas for The Resilience Project. Thankfully, when it came time for Club 21's 2020 Christmas lunch, our Melbourne lockdown had been lifted. I was thrilled to get an invite. The lunch was held at a pub in Hawthorn on a Saturday afternoon and as I headed out the door I told Penny I'd be back in about an hour. When I arrived at the pub I made a beeline for the corner where a big group of people was gathered around a cluster of tables: the members of Club 21.

'Excuse me but this is a private function,' one of the guys said as I went to take a seat.

'Yeah, I know,' I said. 'I was invited.'

Looking around the tables I only recognised one or two faces of the thirty or so who were looking back at me.

It turns out there were two different groups in Club 21, and I had mistakenly been given the date of the second group's Christmas party!

'Who invited you?' the guy asked.

'I'm Hugh,' I said. 'I've been speaking with your friends in Club 21 all year.'

Suddenly a female voice cut through the hum of conversation that filled the room. 'He can stay,' she said. 'He's hot.'

It was like starting from scratch with Club 21. I introduced myself to the group one by one and wished them all a merry Christmas. We then began swapping stories about our hobbies and interests. After half an hour I thought I'd better check in with Penny who was at home with the kids. I went out to the car where I'd left my phone. When I pulled it out of my bag I got a shock.

Nearly three hours had passed.

So, if you want to let go of your addiction to social media, make time for your flow, immerse yourself in it, and enjoy the escape it brings.

EGO

CHAPTER 13
RUNNING

I first heard of Catriona Bisset while thumbing through the sports pages of the *Herald-Sun* in the winter of 2019. As a big athletics fan I was thrilled to learn that she'd broken a record that had stood for forty-three years while competing at the London Diamond League. Catriona's time of 1:58.78 earnt her the title of fastest ever Australian woman over 800 metres.

The newspaper story went on to describe how Catriona, then 25 years old, had quit running in her late teens after she became overwhelmed by anxiety, depression and an eating disorder. At 22 she resumed running after a psychologist suggested it would be good for her mental health. She was soon competing and eventually ran all the way into the history books.

When I put down the newspaper I knew I had to meet this person.

I sent her a DM through Instagram, apologising for the informal approach, but telling her I co-hosted a podcast called *The Imperfects*. 'I wonder if you'd be up for appearing as a guest and unpacking your story?'

To my surprise she said yes. When she returned from her record-setting run in London we met for a coffee and discussed her story, and what a good fit it was for *The Imperfects*. As we exchanged notes on our respective journeys I was struck by her insight and honesty. She was a deep thinker, and no topic was off limits.

'Are you into running at all?' she asked towards the end of our chat.

'Yeah, believe it or not I'm actually into athletics, I'm a sprinter,' I said a bit self-consciously.

'You do?' she asked with a faint note of incredulity, most likely because of my age (I was 38 at the time).

'Yep, I compete every Saturday,' I said. 'I love it.'

I'd taken up running the previous year following my

retirement from a lifetime of cricket. Although I'd done athletics at high school, I never thought I'd do it again but there I was, bolting headlong into middle age, 400 metres at a time.

Having trained by myself for a year, though, during 2019 I'd begun to lose motivation. As I talked this over with Catriona we realised we both ran for the same club, Melbourne University.

'So what time do you run your 400 in?' she asked.

'Fifty-five seconds,' I said, knowing it was a respectable time but nowhere near Catriona's standard.

'You should come and train with us,' she said.

'Er, who's "us"?' I asked.

'The girls I train with,' she said. 'We're coached by Peter Fortune.'

Yeah, no worries, I thought. Just Peter Fortune, personal coach of Cathy Freeman. I'll rock up at your next session and introduce myself, shall I?

'A few of us are pretty focused on Tokyo,' Catriona continued. 'It's a really great group and I think you'd get a lot out of it.'

'You've gotta be kidding me,' I said, smiling in a way that invited her to stop pulling my leg.

'Why not?' she said. 'You'll probably be able to keep up.

If you can't, you'll learn to pretty quickly, and you'll get heaps fitter along the way. They're such a great group of girls, you'll love them.'

From discussing a podcast to being invited to train with future Olympians was a fairly steep ascent. On the one hand it was a dream come true: a personal backstage pass to the world of elite sport. On the other hand it was terrifying. A 38-year-old novice has no place training alongside some of the best athletes in Australia. It would be physically brutal, emotionally risky and potentially humiliating. My ego wanted nothing to do with it.

'I don't know, I'll have to think about it,' I said, having already decided there was no way in the world I'd consider it. My ego was now barking loudly in my ear: You'll look like a fool. You've got nothing to prove anyway. You're quicker than most blokes your age. Why would you subject yourself to humiliation? You're better than that.

'Don't think about it, just do it!' Catriona said. 'You've got nothing to lose.'

'Oh, I don't know about that,' I shot back with a pained expression on my face.

Catriona said her squad would be training at Lakeside Stadium the following Tuesday. 'We'll be doing ten 200-metre sprints with two minutes' rest in between. The aim is to do them in around twenty-seven seconds each. If you reckon you can manage that, you should turn up.'

EGO IS NOT A DIRTY WORD

Eckhart Tolle, one of the world's great philosophers, defines ego as 'identification with form, primarily thought forms'. If I let go of my ego for a second I'm happy to admit I have no idea what that means. I much prefer the definition given by Ryan Holiday, bestselling author of *Ego Is the Enemy*. He calls ego 'an unhealthy belief in our own importance'. He says it turns a concern we have about ourselves into an obsession, and a healthy confidence into arrogance.

Think of ego as the custodian and narrator of the story of who we think we should be. It talks to us all day long, reiterating our self-image by repeating the same stories with the same subtext, over and over again. Our ego is set up to try to protect us from harm – be it embarrassment, shame or disappointment – but problems arise when we get stuck in our stories and mentally straitjacketed when there are opportunities to learn and grow.

Had I listened solely to my ego after I had coffee with Catriona I'd have gone straight home and blown off the invitation to train. I have nothing to prove. What's the point? I don't want to look like a fool for no reason . . .

Rather than pay heed to my ego, however, I drove to Collingwood Athletics Track that afternoon and put myself through Catriona's Olympic training drill. My love of running and my fascination with elite sport caused me to be vulnerable instead of egotistical.

When I'd completed the ten lots of 200-metre sprints I collapsed into the foetal position and tried desperately not to throw up. I was completely cooked but, by pushing myself to the limit, I'd managed to run 200 metres in an average of twenty-nine seconds – two seconds shy of the female Olympic hopefuls.

I began to seriously consider Catriona's invitation. I figured the adrenaline and nerves I'd likely feel on the day might almost be enough to compensate for the two-second lag. Maybe I wouldn't crash and burn after all.

When Tuesday rolled around I could hardly concentrate at work. I swung wildly between vulnerability and egotism: committing to the session, willing to fail, and not turning up to save myself the embarrassment. I was still debating what to do when I jumped in my car. Just drive to the track and sit in the carpark, I told myself. You can make your mind up when you get there.

As soon as I arrived at Lakeside Stadium, even before I pulled on the handbrake, I saw Catriona climbing off her bike. More significantly, she saw me. 'Uh oh, this is actually going to happen,' I murmured.

'Hey!' she said with a wave. 'Are you ready to train?'

A few minutes later Catriona used her official pass to swipe us into the Victorian Institute of Sport's impressive Albert Park facility.

'It's pretty easy-going,' she said as my wide eyes took it all in. 'It's just me and the girls and we really just stick to our program. Very straightforward.'

As we walked onto the beautiful blue track, the first person I saw was the fastest man in Australia over 800 metres, Peter Bol, in full stride and shirtless with all ten abs on display. I looked down at my dad bod, in a T-shirt and trackie dacks, and wondered what the hell I was doing there.

Catriona introduced me to Peter Fortune and 'the girls' – eight athletes aged 18 to 26, with a total of eighty impressive abs between them. They were welcoming and warm but I could tell they were focused on the task ahead.

Whenever I trained, my warm-up consisted of a lap of the track followed by some stretches. When Catriona finished with the introductions the girls set off on *their* version of a warm-up. Still wearing my tracksuit pants, and with my phone bouncing around in my pocket, I followed them. After a surprisingly short distance I started breathing hard and struggled to keep up. Meanwhile, I could hear the girls chatting to each other breezily about life and work as if they were on a gentle stroll through a park.

'So how long is this warm-up run?' I panted.

'Oh, probably about four kilometres,' came the reply.

I considered stopping right there and crawling back to my car. Had someone asked me before the session, 'Can you run four kilometres in sixteen minutes?' I'd have laughed and said, 'Nah. Not possible.' But somehow I hung on, phone bouncing in my pocket all the way back to the stadium.

At that point I really did just want to go home. I considered feigning an injury as I folded in half with my hands on my knees, trying to breathe normally. Meanwhile, the girls acted like they'd just stepped off a tram.

Next up were the ten 200-metre sprints in twenty-seven seconds or less. As I'd hoped, either the adrenaline or the sense of occasion gave me a spark that allowed me to continue. I managed to complete eight sprints in around twenty-seven seconds.

Two to go, I encouraged myself. Then, out of nowhere,

my legs started twitching and shaking uncontrollably, as if I'd been plugged into a 240-volt socket. All I could think to do to alleviate the bizarre electrocution was lie on my back and stick my feet in the air. It must have been an extraordinary sight for onlookers. Eight of the fittest young women in Australia awaiting their next sprint effort with a middle-aged man lying on his back with his legs reaching for the sky. Somehow, it worked (a little) and I managed to get back on my feet and complete the last two sprints. I was a fair way off the pace but by that point I didn't care. With the drill done I collapsed on the lush grass beside the track, overcome by a euphoria I'd never experienced before. I'd encountered the benefits of endorphins in the past but this was one of the most exquisite sensations I'd ever felt.

As I floated on this cloud of peptides the great Peter Fortune addressed the squad. 'Okay,' he said, 'that was really good. Now, we're going to finish with a 400.'

In an instant my sense of euphoria was gone.

'I'm not sure that's physically possible,' I said.

Peter ignored the remark. 'Hugh,' he said, 'I need you to go out in front of Catriona and pace her. You need to stay in front of her, okay?'

'I couldn't stay in front of her if she was walking!' I cried.

It didn't seem to register with the coach. 'Thanks Hugh,' he said.

We set off and I managed to follow Peter's instructions – for all of three metres. As the girls flew past me I decided it was okay to complete this final lap in my own time. I felt like I was on some kind of victory lap: I wasn't exactly waving at people in the stands but I wasn't far off it.

As I entered the back straight the feelings of bliss returned. Why do I feel so unbelievably alive and happy? I wondered. Obviously the endorphins had played a part but there was definitely something else going on. Maybe it was the connection I felt with these people. They'd been supportive and empathetic as I battled to keep up with them. Perhaps it was the fact I'd embraced my imperfections: the perception of myself as an ageing man in the presence of youth and vitality. Maybe it was the vulnerability I had needed to even be at the session. All of these reasons played a part but the main reason I felt so good, I decided, was that I'd let go of my ego and parked it at the door.

Before I could think any more of it, one of the girls shouted, 'Righto, let's do a quick four kilometres to recover!'

Will this ever end? I thought and staggered off after them.

■

I returned for more sessions with the Olympics-bound Aussies but when COVID-19's tentacles spread through Melbourne in 2020, I figured it was all over. The athletes were still allowed to train but not in a group. They were limited to one training partner each and had to remain 1.5 metres apart. I was stunned when Catriona Bisset asked me to be her training partner for a number of sessions. I thought the day would eventually come when Peter Fortune took me aside and said, 'It's been nice having you but I need her to be surrounded by elite athletes.'

Strangely, that moment never came.

Since my role was to 'pace' Catriona, Peter had me start five metres in front of her. Instead of keeping up, she had to chase me down. Which she always did.

There were plenty of people Catriona Bisset could have trained with so naturally I puzzled over why I was in the mix. It turned out it was all about friendship and camaraderie. Unlike team sports, running is a fairly lonely pursuit. When I look back on my cricketing days I don't think about the premierships won or wickets taken – I reflect on the personal connections and the lifelong friendships that were forged.

I wasn't there to enhance Catriona's speed, I was there for the laughter, the conversations and to celebrate the imperfections of the journey with her. Our unlikely friendship reminded me of the power of vulnerability and the positivity of connection.

In my final race of the 2021 season I beat my personal best time, running 400 metres in fifty-two seconds. Catriona was the first person I called. As she encouraged me to relive the moment with her over the phone, I felt a deep sense of gratitude that I'd let go of my ego that day when she first invited me to Lakeside Stadium. Training with 'the girls' had opened a door to immense personal growth.

It also left me – through no fault of theirs – with a very unhealthy obsession with body image.

Aside from getting to chat with amazing guests like Catriona Bisset, *The Imperfects* podcast has been a great vehicle for exploring concepts such as ego, shame, vulnerability and expectation.

Ryan, Josh and I invented a game off the back of a pun Ryan had come up with for a segment called 'The Vulnerabili-Tea-House'. To encourage people to explore vulnerability, we pretend we're hanging out at a tea house. Josh found good tea house music which we play as we sit in the studio and, you get it, drink tea. The game centres on a set of cards on which are written different questions that encourage vulnerability. We take turns drawing three cards and choosing one question to answer. While the aim of the game is primarily to model vulnerability, I've realised we are also modelling how to *receive* vulnerability.

The first card I drew in the Vulnerabili-Tea-House asked, 'In which part of your life do you still feel lonely?'

'Jesus, that's heavy,' I said with a sigh.

The second question was, 'What did it take you too long to learn about yourself?'

Yeah, I could say a few things about that, I thought.

But when I pulled the third card I knew I had to confront an uncomfortable truth. 'What's the first thing you see when you look in the mirror?'

The question was open to interpretation: perhaps it was an invitation to explore my inner self. Did I see a father in the mirror? Did I see an older version of the boy I used to be? Did I see a success or a failure?

Instead, I chose to take the question literally – and be completely honest.

For many years the first thing I saw when I looked in the mirror was my hair. It had started thinning when I was about 19, triggering a crisis of confidence that lasted the best part of twenty years. I spent a lot of time in front of the mirror, stressing out and trying to hide the fact I was going bald prematurely (a fair bit of ego at play right there).

For many years I grew the front of my hair long and swept it into a fringe of sorts. That was fine, so long as it wasn't windy. For ten years I entered rooms and auditoriums around the country while pretending to scratch my head. In reality I was holding my hair down so it didn't blow around and reveal my great cranial shame.

In early 2021 I turned up at my barber's for my regular trim. A trusted co-conspirator, he'd been in on the 'Hugh hair deception' for many years and knew just how I liked it cut. He was on holiday on this particular day so I had to submit to the scissors of his replacement. He was an affable chap and although his English wasn't that good he seemed to understand when I held up a thumb and forefinger indicating I wanted about an inch removed. He nodded and smiled, then grabbed my precious fringe as if it were a ponytail and chopped it clean off.

'*Nooo!*' I screamed, turning heads in the salon and leaving the poor barber shocked (but not quite as shocked as me). It was a simple misunderstanding: he thought I wanted my hair to be an inch long all over, not trimmed back *by* an inch.

There was no going back, though. He finished the job and I left the shop dazed and discombobulated, like a freshly shorn spring lamb. Feeling naked and utterly exposed, I scurried to my car with one hand covering my balding pate, trying to pretend to the world it was business as usual up top at Hugh's.

A week later I could not have cared less. I had become comfortable with my limited bonce. Not only did I no longer have to fixate on it in the mirror every morning, but I didn't have to worry when I went for a swim, or a run, or whether it was windy or not. Most of all I took pride and comfort in the fact I was finally being honest about my hair. In that respect my ego had been silenced. It'd finally been let go. If only I'd met that replacement barber when I was 20! I might have saved myself a truckload of angst and thousands of dollars in hair growth pills and sticky product.

So while for most of my life the answer to the question on the Vulnerabili-Tea-House card 'What's the first thing you see when you look in the mirror?' would have been 'my hair', I now realised I had to confront and talk about a new obsession.

Even worse, it was one I'd never shared before.

After training with the Olympians, I simply could not stop looking at my stomach. The sessions were so intense that for the first time in my life I developed something approaching a six-pack – a standard physical feature among high-performance runners. It must be said that at the time of writing (age 41), my abs were the best they had ever been.

Rather than being chuffed about this by-product of serious exercise, I became extremely critical of it. One day Josh caught me lifting my shirt up at work and staring at my stomach – literally navel-gazing.

'What are you doing?' he said with an expression on his face you can probably imagine.

'I don't understand why my stomach doesn't look like the people I run with,' I lamented.

'Because you're not a twenty-two-year-old female Olympic track athlete,' Josh said.

'No, no, I'm talking about the *guys* who train there,' I said. 'Those guys have all got full-on ten-packs!'

Aside from my hair, I had never struggled with body issues. During my formative years 'body issues' were wrongly considered a problem that only affected females. Well, it's now estimated males account for 25–40 per cent of people with eating disorders.

I'd been active in sport for my entire life but it took training with the best in the country to bring on this attack of the vapours over how my body appeared. After the

COVID-19 lockdowns ended and normal training resumed I brought the subject up with the girls.

'So here is an interesting topic I'd like to discuss,' I began.

'Fire away,' they said.

'Well, I'm starting to think way too much about how I look – especially my stomach,' I said. 'I'm constantly gawking at it and it's starting to freak me out that I care so much.'

'Er, yeah!'

'We all do that!'

'Hello!'

After this chorus of responses they also admitted they compared their physiques to other athletes. I was relieved I wasn't the only one. I'd become fixated on the cartoonishly proportioned body of US hurdler Kerron Clement (google his abs). I told myself that only when my abdominals matched Kerron's could I be happy with them.

Having seen my sister endure the horrors of an eating disorder when she was a teenager, I've been acutely aware of the importance of a nutritious and balanced diet my entire life. But soon I started obsessing over food, too. The first sign of a problem was when it started to impinge on my favourite day of the week.

Every Sunday morning I take Benji to the Queen Victoria Market to queue up for Australia's most delicious donuts, sold from an old-school American food van that has been parked there since the 1950s. It's both a Melbourne and van Cuylenburg institution: Mum and Dad used to take me there when I was a kid. Sometimes the queue stretches for eighty metres, but we don't care – the wait is always worth it.

Normally I'd buy two donuts for Benji and tell him I was having two as well, but I'd actually get four for myself. I'd then grab one of the city's best brews from Market Lane Coffee and a babycino for Benji. We'd sit in the sun on the same bench, my arm around his shoulders as we ate our donuts and watched the world drift by.

As Mum pointed out that day in the park, one of my jobs as a dad is to make memories for my children, and since the donut van loomed large in the sepia of my childhood, I thought the least I could do was pass it down to Benji. He was always excited to go to the market and it was by far the time of the week I looked forward to most – until I started stressing over the donuts.

Shit – this thing's going to make me run slower, I'd think as I lifted another clump of scrumptious, sugar-crusted dough to my lips. It will ruin my abs!

Shut up! the rational part of my brain would snap. This *isn't* about you. This is about your son. He's not going to look back and think, Dad ruined his abs eating donuts here.

Nowadays I'm having just two donuts. As soon as they're finished the inner argument starts all over again.

I want another one, rational Hugh will say.

It'll go straight to your abs! my ego will bite back.

Who cares, you're 41. Eat five friggin' donuts!

This is absolutely not a conversation I expected to be having with myself at my age. Yet, here I am.

I guess I'm only human.

CHAPTER 14

LESSONS FROM MY DAD

Over the years many people have praised me for sticking with The Resilience Project in the early days when I was struggling to get it off the ground. I even wrote a chapter, 'Minus one coffee', in my last book, to highlight how touch-and-go it was back then. What I didn't mention were the three occasions I all but gave it away and applied for a job somewhere else. The reason? Ego.

Worried my start-up would fail, I sought full-time employment at Cricket Australia, Cricket Victoria and Headspace, the national non-profit that focuses on youth mental health. When I was turned down by each organisation I was inwardly shattered. But instead of projecting vulnerability, I pretended I was angry because my ego couldn't cope with the rejection. I told myself and anyone who'd listen it was the organisations that had screwed up, not me.

This, of course, was nonsense. Take the Headspace interview. I'd applied for a position as head of school programs, and part of the interview required me to read a mock media report relating to a Headspace program. 'Okay, you'll have five minutes to read this article,' said the lady conducting the interview. 'When I come back, I want you to discuss how you'd deal with the issues raised in it.'

When she left the room I tried to read it but halfway through the first paragraph my mind went for a wander. How am I going so far? I thought to myself. This is a nice building. I wonder where my office will be. Will I get an office? Or maybe it's a hot-desking situation . . .

For five full minutes I was stuck in a mental vacuum: my eyes were seeing the words on the page but not a single one registered.

The door eventually opened and the lady returned. 'Okay,' she said brightly, 'let's discuss the article.'

I wish there was an audio recording of my answer. It

would make hilarious listening because I actually tried to give some thoughts and insight on an article I hadn't read! In hindsight the look of total confusion on the poor woman's face was priceless, too.

Although I didn't get the job, Headspace offered me feedback on what I could do to better position myself for a role in the future. I reacted to this very kind, sensible offer by saying, 'Nah, don't worry about.'

Arrogant.

Defensive.

Dripping with ego.

Later that night I told Mum and Dad what had happened. 'I'm pretty glad I didn't get the job to be honest,' I said over dinner. 'I didn't have a great feeling about the place. Something wasn't right.'

Yeah, you bet something wasn't right. His name was Hugh. I sometimes wonder what story the lady who interviewed me told *her* parents that night. Were it not for my ego, I would have sat down with the people at Headspace and likely learnt how to improve myself.

Like many of us, my ego would rear its head whenever I felt insecure or unsure of myself. It would try to protect me from harm (embarrassment and shame) but in the long run it was a handbrake on my progress in life. During my first year teaching I felt extremely insecure. As a result I never once sought advice from my more experienced colleagues. My ego wanted everyone to think I knew exactly what I was doing.

Perhaps my best example of self-sabotage by ego occurred when I was 22. I'd somehow found myself hosting a weekly cricket show on Melbourne's SEN radio station. Despite the fact I was terrible at it, I received a phone call out of the blue from a man asking if I'd be interested in being the ground announcer at the upcoming Victoria vs Tasmania cricket match, which was to be broadcast on Channel Nine. I couldn't believe my luck. It was a dream opportunity: a potential door into the world of cricket broadcasting.

When the day arrived my nerves were shot as I ascended the grandstand at The Junction Oval and took a seat in the media box, surrounded by seasoned match officials. Apart from pretending to be Bill Lawry when I self-commentated games of backyard cricket as a boy, I had no experience whatsoever as an announcer. I felt desperately unsure of myself and right on cue my ego arrived to make sure I did a woeful job.

'I'm happy to sit with you and help you out if you don't know what you're doing,' said the lovely older gent who'd been assigned to look after me. Upon hearing this, the nearby officials spun around to hear my response. What I should have said was, 'I have no idea what I'm doing here. Please sit down and don't leave my side.'

My ego, however, decided to answer the question. 'Thanks mate, I've got this.'

Well, I didn't have it. I made a mess of the job and a fool of myself. As Australian batting legend Michael Bevan strode out to the crease to take his mark I was so overwhelmed with the information being fed to me that I butchered his name. 'The incoming batsman for the Tasmanian Tigers is . . . Michael Heaven!' I yelled over the ground's PA. I covered my mouth in shock and I swear everyone at the ground (including Michael Heaven) turned to look at me.

While I did a fairly awful job that day I was aware I'd somehow been given a valuable foot in the door. Deep down I'd have loved to be part of that scene and as I was packing up to leave, the lovely older man wandered over and offered me a second chance. 'Definite room for improvement,' he said, 'but we'd be happy to have you back. You've got my number so give me a call if you'd like to have another go.'

I kept his number on my bedside table for months and thought about calling him every day. But I never did. Eventually I threw the number away. My ego couldn't handle the thought of not being 'perfect' at something straight off the bat while I learnt the ropes. It was the same voice that, sixteen years later, told me not to turn up to train with the Olympians. I wonder if I'd ignored my ego at the age of 22, where life might have taken me.

It's no wonder legendary US basketball coach Pat Riley calls ego 'the disease of me'. Another American sporting great, four-time undefeated mixed martial arts world champion Frank Shamrock, goes even further. 'False ideas about yourself destroy you.'

Shamrock says he managed to stay on top in one of the world's most intensely competitive sports because he relied on a system of checks and balances that stopped him from developing an ego. Shamrock calls his approach 'plus, minus, equal'.[1]

PLUS, MINUS, EQUAL
Plus – *learn from someone who is more experienced than you*

One of the most foolhardy things we can do is approach life believing we already know everything we need to know. My arrogant rejection of help from the older man in the media box was a good example of how far that mentality will get you. If we don't listen to people who know more than we do, we'll find it very hard to learn. There is always someone who knows more and has more experience than us. It might be a mentor, a coach, a colleague or a teammate. Look for them and listen to them.

Minus – *teach someone less experienced than you*

It is impossible to teach without first learning. Through educating or instructing those less knowledgeable, we are forced to consolidate our higher understanding. We will always learn something when we have to pull apart a topic in order to explain it to someone else. Be alert to people who are willing to learn from you and seize the opportunity – it's a win-win.

Equal – *engage with someone with the same experience as you*

Competition is a great leveller. It's also a great motivator. That's why it's important to seek out and connect with people who challenge us. There's a reason Catriona Bisset and the girls train together, even though as runners they're in direct competition with one another. As equals and rivals they push each other towards

> greater results and learn from each other along the way. The same dynamics apply in all walks of life. If there's an area in which you want to improve, seek out your equals.

The 'plus, minus, equal' approach to ego control has been of great benefit to me. It's the reason I ended up training with the Olympians – my willingness to learn (plus). But I have to say having kids was the final nail in the coffin of my ego. Nowadays, I'm entirely comfortable with insecurity and feeling unsure of myself. After all, it is a normal, rational state of mind. I can't say I've managed to completely let go of all ego, but I'm on my way.

In a session with my psychologist Anita towards the end of 2020, she asked me how I'd like my children to talk about me when they're older. While I think she meant it as a question to go away and ponder, I responded in a heartbeat. 'Humble and kind,' I stated emphatically. 'I hope my kids see me as humble and kind.'

Answering Anita's question is another great tool to help put your ego in check. I'm aware not everyone becomes a parent so Ben Crowe has a variation of the same question: 'When you die, what two words would you hope people use to describe you in their eulogy?'

Now that you know what mine are, think about *your* two words. When you know what they are, write them down and put them where you'll always see them: on the fridge, on the dashboard of your car; use them as a password for your computer or make them the screen saver on your phone. When you feel insecure, unsure or even frightened about a choice you have to make, go to these words to guide your actions.

Do not consult your ego.

Since establishing 'humble' and 'kind' as my go-to words, I've noticed myself saying the following a lot more:

- I don't know.
- You're right.
- I'm not an expert.
- Sorry.
- Thank you.

I think the whole world could get better at saying these things, especially in uncertain times like these.

As I was nearing the end of writing this book I had a follow-up session with Anita. 'Tell me more about these words "humble and kind",' she said. 'Where do they come from? Why do they mean so much to you?'

I knew the answer straight away, just as I'd known

243

immediately what the words were when she'd first asked. But this time I struggled to say it out loud. Each time I went to open my mouth I thought I might burst into tears. Eventually I managed a response. 'They're about my dad,' I said, my voice cracking with emotion. 'I want to be just like Dad.'

In my twenty-first and final season of premier cricket we were lucky enough to make the finals. On day one of the semifinal, on a fresh autumn morning, I noticed an older man with white hair walking around the perimeter taking in the day's play. A few minutes later it dawned on me that the old bloke was my father. For the first time I was struck by the realisation this towering figure in my life was mortal. Oh my God, I thought. He looks *old*. In that moment I felt an overwhelming compulsion to have children.

As soon as I got home I discussed it with Penny. At the time we had plans to spend a few years living and working in New York before returning to Melbourne to start a family. 'That was our deal! It's been a dream of mine for a very long time,' Penny said, a little surprised I suddenly wanted to change the script.

'I know, I know,' I said. 'But you should have seen him

today. He looked more like a grandfather, and I don't want him to miss out on having grandkids.'

Penny considered this point. 'That's a very good reason to start a family,' she agreed. 'I guess we can always travel after we have kids.'

About a year later, Dad was one of the first people to hold our son Benji and welcome him into the world.

I talked a lot about Dad during my sessions with Anita, particularly about my emotional reaction to him getting older. My dad, Richard van Cuylenburg, hails from a family of Dutch Burghers from Sri Lanka who set sail for a new start in Australia when he was nine years old. His parents and brother weren't as dark-skinned as Dad. There was a concern that his complexion would run afoul of the White Australia Policy of the day – so much so that Dad was told to stay indoors for two weeks before the family embarked on the journey to Australia.

Whether Australian immigration officially deemed Dad to be not so dark as to disqualify him, I do not know. At any rate, he was allowed into the country in 1957, where his skin colour and thick accent guaranteed he was subjected to less formal but just as damaging types of racial abuse and discrimination.

Throughout his formative years as a 'new Australian' Dad was marginalised and mocked for his 'otherness'. But like so many other migrants, he tucked his chin in, put his head down and wrung every last chance out of the opportunity he'd been given. In Dad's mind it was his guiding responsibility to honour his parents, who'd given up everything in Sri Lanka so he and his brother could make a better life for themselves. No amount of name-calling, belittling or social ostracisation was going to make Dad forget that.

When I was a boy my granny enthralled us with stories about how Dad would study from 4 pm until 10 pm every day as a kid. He wouldn't even break for dinner, which she served him in his room. Even after Dad fell in love with Mum when he was in Year 12 (and she was in Year 11), he hit the books for six hours straight every day after school and on the weekend, only allowing himself a ten-minute break to chat to her on the phone.

Dad's hard work saw him admitted to Melbourne University, where he studied dentistry. He began practising at the age of 24 and, after having just one day off sick his entire working life, he retired at 65. In doing so, Dad (with Mum) kicked down the door of the Lucky Country for his own children. He made sure we were given every opportunity he'd been given, and so much more.

Today my parents are my heroes. Dad is everything I aspire to be as a man. As a young boy I looked up to him as a paragon of virtue and a sporting superstar in local cricketing circles. Not only that, he was also a *dentist* and every trip to visit him in his surgery in the city filled me with awe and pride.

My fondest memories, however, revolved around late nights in summer when he let me stay up to watch Australia play One Day Cricket on TV. He'd talk me through every over: the tension and excitement building to a giddy crescendo, especially when it was a close finish. They still rate among the best nights of my life.

But there came a time when others started to compete for a spot on the pedestal I'd placed him upon. Thanks to Dad's hard work, I was given the opportunity to attend a private secondary school. There I started meeting other kids' dads, who somehow seemed to strut a bit taller, talk a bit louder and cast a shadow over my humble, kind and diligent father.

For a while I became convinced the other dads were cooler than mine. They had a lot of money and no shame in flashing it around. Share portfolios and holiday homes were casually discussed on the sidelines of our school sports days by sleek, confident and extroverted men. Why can't Dad be more like them? I'd wonder whenever I was in the company of these upper-class players.

School pick-up time at Carey Grammar saw a fleet of foreign cars descend upon the school gates: BMWs, Mercedes, Jaguars and Audis. Meanwhile, our family plied the streets in an old Mitsubishi station wagon. Dad couldn't have cared less about what badge was on the bonnet – all he wanted in a car was a means of getting from A to B. Whenever I got a lift home with a mate's dad, however, I'd sit in the car on the soft leather seats and secretly wish we had a BMW, too.

In 1996 I was invited to join a mate's family at their beachside retreat for the summer holidays. On the long drive there my mate's father was pulled over for speeding, just outside Geelong.

'Watch this, boys,' he said as he unbuckled his seatbelt and climbed out of the car. 'See how it's done.'

We observed through the back window as he walked straight up to the policeman, shook his hand and then spread his elbows wide, hands on hips.

After talking with the officer for a minute or two, my friend's dad climbed back into his expensive car and closed the door with a self-satisfied expression on his face. 'And that, boys, is how you do it,' he said. 'You meet them on their own territory, you shake their hand, you look them in the eye and tell them you won't do it again.'

I was extremely impressed.

A few months later Dad and I made our way back to the Mitsubishi at a packed shopping centre to find a parking inspector sliding a ticket under the windscreen wiper. Dad apologised profusely to the inspector. 'I am in the wrong,' he said. 'I deserve that ticket.'

As we headed for home I thought, There's no way my mate's dad would have put up with that for a second. He'd have talked his way out of it.

Thank God we tend to gain more insight as we grow older. By the time I was in my twenties I felt the same way about Dad as I'd done as a boy, on the couch with him late at night, glued to the cricket. I am so proud of his quiet grace and grateful for his and Mum's steady and loving steward-ship of our family.

As I closed in on 40, my love for Dad emerged as a major topic during my sessions with Anita. More specifically, how I *felt* about Dad became a primary focus of my therapy. I carried a lot of shame about the attitude I'd had towards him when I was a teenager. I was sickened by the fact I'd wished him to be something that he wasn't, as if he weren't enough just as he was.

Anita showed me a graphic called the 'power and privilege wheel'. It's essentially a pie chart with power and privilege positioned at the centre. The circle is divided into segments rating different characteristics including skin colour, gender, country of birth, education, wealth, mental health, language, and so on. The less power and privilege you have, the further from the centre of the wheel you fall.

'I want you to look at that chart and show me where your dad was positioned as a boy getting off the boat and arriving in Australia,' Anita said.

I plotted his results and realised, for the first time, that for much of Dad's life he was on the far outskirts of where power, privilege and entitlement exist in Australia. His was not a comfortable place in the social strata.

'Now have a look where you fall on the wheel,' Anita said.

I was slap-bang in the centre: a veritable bullseye of privilege, power and entitlement. And I had not arrived there by accident. Dad had spent most of his life working to bring his children in from the fringes of the privilege wheel and lay incredible opportunities at our feet; the same opportunities that he had to scratch and claw towards, beginning with studying for forty-two hours a week.

'You would have seen many parents at your school who were in the middle of the wheel, wouldn't you?' Anita asked.

'Yeah, everywhere,' I said.

'Can you describe some of the typical characteristics and traits of those people, the ones at the centre of the wheel?'

'Arrogant,' I began. 'Selfish. Disrespectful. Dishonest. Entitled . . .'

'Right,' she said. 'Now give me the characteristics that would describe someone who is *not* privileged, who is *not* entitled.'

'Oh, humble, hard-working, kind, selfless, honest . . .'

'You've just described your father, haven't you?' she said.

'Absolutely,' I said, as tears started to roll down my cheeks.

Dad had arrived in Australia with nothing. Everything he had came through hard work, and he did it all for his family. He was never going to try to talk a parking officer out of giving him a fine. He knew he'd done the wrong thing and that was the price to be paid. Since he wasn't privileged, he had a rational view of the way the world works. He'd made his own way – within the rules – and he didn't feel comfortable owing anyone anything.

I left the session with Anita that day adamant that I wanted my children to be like my dad. They'd been born at the centre of the power and privilege wheel, too, but only through the Herculean efforts of their grandfather. When I'd seen him at the cricket looking old that day I thought

I wanted to have kids so he wouldn't miss out on meeting his grandchildren. Anita helped me uncover the real reason – I didn't want my children to miss out on meeting him.

AFTERWORD

One of my all-time favourite family photos dates from Christmas 2014 when we rented an Airbnb in Fairhaven on Victoria's majestic Surf Coast. I'd been dating Penny for just two weeks and she'd stopped by for a few days but for the most part, it was just Mum, Dad, Georgia, Josh and me, blissfully soaking up the sun. The photograph – snapped on the balcony of our rented beach house – captured all of us in our element: the three 'kids' deep in conversation, Dad reading a book, half-listening, and Mum watching over us all. It perfectly distilled all of the happiest weeks of my life. Naturally, being me, I wanted to recreate it.

After a year of lockdowns that had stopped us seeing much of Mum and Dad, I was desperate to reunite the family for a much-needed escape. There would be some new faces this time around, too: our children Benji and Elsie, plus their adorable cousin Charlie, the first child of Josh and his partner Sophie. The only person missing would be Georgia, who was stuck in America thanks to closed borders.

In early 2021 I found a house in Fairhaven for the upcoming Easter long weekend. I spent every single day of the next two months looking forward to it. We all did. By then I'd come to terms with the fact I didn't have to light up every room I walked into, so I just wanted to relax with my family and be a good dad to the kids and a good uncle to Charlie.

We arrived on Easter Friday on a perfect day: 30 degrees, sunny and with a gentle breeze floating in off the sapphire sea. I felt like I'd stepped into the family photo album and my beloved picture from years before. The kids woke us up early on Easter Saturday so Josh and I joined them on the balcony to feast on hot cross buns and watch the ochre sunrise over Bass Strait. The morning was even more beautiful than I'd hoped it would be. While my little brother took in the magnificent scene, I looked lovingly at him and made a mental note to remember this moment for as long as I lived.

As the carefree sand-and-sunscreen-encrusted day wore on I noticed little Charlie started to develop a bit of a sneeze.

Around sunset Benji was sneezing and coughing, too. By bedtime Elsie had joined in with a coughing and snot show of her own. No one got much in the way of uninterrupted sleep that night as we played bedtime whack-a-mole with the teary and irritably sick children.

Day three dawned warm and orange once again, promising another perfect day on the continent's spectacular southern fringe. Everyone shared a laugh about our lack of proper sleep and I reminded myself it was the imperfections that made life memorable. Besides, we'd all get a great sleep that night.

Around lunchtime the hot water system gave out just as the weather deteriorated and the temperature plunged from 30 to 15 degrees. A steady drizzle settled on Fairhaven, turning the sparkling beach into a damp and misty ghost town. By mid-afternoon one of the toilets stopped working, leaving just one loo between nine people and causing stress levels to creep up a notch.

Still, I remained philosophical. Life doesn't have to be perfect, I told myself. I'm just happy we're all here together.

Everyone was exhausted on Sunday night and heads indeed hit pillows early. Still struggling with the sniffles, Charlie woke up crying about 11.30 pm. In the small, open-plan beach house, that meant everyone woke up at 11.30 pm.

As soon as Sophie and Josh got Charlie back to sleep Elsie began screaming, and she kept it up from midnight until 3 am. Knowing everyone was awake and stressing out about our screaming child, I became decidedly less philosophical than I'd been. Okay, things are not supposed to be perfect, I thought. This is a *fucking nightmare*!

I managed to get Elsie back down around 3 am and as I drifted off around 4 am Benji – who was in the bed between me and Penny – started to cough uncontrollably. In a terrifying turn he sat bolt upright and grabbed at his throat as if struggling to breathe. His cough morphed into something more like a dog barking and choking at the same time. Depressingly, we'd seen this before with Benji: it was croup.

This attack, however, was a whopper. Benji threw himself across the bed and lay on his back gasping for air. Desperate to catch a breath he tried to reach down his throat with his little hands to open up his airways. It was a horrifying thing to behold and unlike anything we'd seen before.

'Call an ambulance,' Penny instructed.

I was already on the case, fumbling for my phone.

When Benji heard the word 'ambulance' he freaked out and grew even worse. Our darling boy writhed in pain and terror as his body cried out for oxygen it just couldn't get. I was distraught, fully convinced he was dying.

The nearest ambulance station was in Anglesea and it took forty minutes to arrive. In the meantime Penny tried to calm Benji by rocking him in her arms while I waited at the end of the driveway in my boxers and a T-shirt, panicking in the cold and dark. The rest of the household was awake and equally distressed about what was happening.

Just after 5 am the paramedics took him to hospital in Geelong. Penny rode along in the back of the ambulance, leaving me to watch over Elsie and try to pick up the pieces of our shattered family holiday.

Around 6.30 am Penny phoned from the hospital to say Benji had been stabilised, was doing fine and would I come and collect them. When I climbed behind the wheel and turned the key, the car came alive with Ben Crowe's voice. I'd been listening to the latest episode of *The Imperfects* when we'd arrived three days earlier. Now the recording had resumed where I'd left off, just in the right place for some insightful advice: 'You can't control life, it's completely uncertain and unpredictable . . . if you try to control things you can't control you spend your whole life frustrated, but once you embrace uncertainty in the way you embrace imperfection . . .'

At St John hospital in Geelong I was beyond relieved to see my son breathing normally, with colour in his cheeks and a tired grin on his face. Shattered from the emotional trauma and lack of sleep, Penny and I smiled weakly at each other, too. The joy of the past few days seemed to have ebbed away like an outgoing tide but all we cared about was that our little boy was safe and well.

The following day we packed up at Fairhaven and headed for home. We'd taken two cars down the coast and decided to divide and conquer for the two-hour return trip, too. Penny teamed up with Elsie, and Benji came with me. We chatted about his visit to the hospital, and as we cruised east along the Princes Freeway, I found myself thinking about a recent conversation I'd had with Anita.

'I can't handle mess,' I'd confessed. 'We have two kids and when I get home from work the house is a bombsite. So I spend two and a half hours cleaning up every single night. I can't stop myself!'

'Why do you think that is?' she asked.

'I just need the house to be perfect when I wake up in the morning,' I said.

'It sounds like the messier your life is the more you want to physically clean the space around you,' Anita said.

'Yeah,' I said, nodding. 'That's probably very true.'

'But Hugh, life is messy!'

'Yeah, I guess it is,' I said, kind of absently.

'No, no, listen,' Anita went on. 'We've been talking for a year now and what I know about you is your life has *always* been messy, and you've worked out a way to get through it each time. It's not that your life has suddenly become messy lately – it has always been that way and it probably always will be. That's just life.'

My reflections on the chaos of humanity were interrupted halfway between Geelong and Melbourne when Benji stirred in his booster seat. 'Daddy, I need to go to the toilet,' he said.

'No worries, mate,' I replied as I pulled onto the shoulder of the freeway.

'I can't go here!' he said, wide-eyed and alarmed that I thought a roadside slash would somehow be okay with him. 'People will see me!'

'Are you sure you're not comfortable going on the side of the road?'

'No,' he said. 'We need to go to McDonovan's.'

I was never allowed to have McDonald's as a kid. In fact, one of my earliest memories is of Mum and Dad saying, 'You're not getting it. *Ever.*'

I trusted they knew what was good for me so I never

questioned their decision. I'd see the Maccas ads on TV, the cast of silly mascots and, of course, we'd driven past a thousand outlets, but I never set foot inside a McDonald's until I was ten years old. The occasion was an end-of-season baseball party. Naturally curious and covetous about the McForbidden fruit after a decade of parental sanctions, I was excited that I'd finally get a taste of one of those burgers, some French fries and a thickshake.

The only problem was that Mum had spoken with the manager after she'd dropped me off. Just as the high-cholesterol orders arrived for all of the other kids in the special party room, a teenage waitress called loudly above the din, 'Where's Hugh?'

When I stuck my hand in the air she skipped over and handed me a cling-wrapped cheese and lettuce sandwich that had been cut into a circle – a sad and disappointing imitation of a McDonald's cheeseburger.

'There you go,' the girl said. 'Your mum said to give you this.'

Like mother, like son. If Benji ever asks for McDonald's (or McDonovan's as he calls it, for reasons best known to himself) on a long car trip I order him a 'Happy Meal'. But instead of chips, he gets tomatoes. Instead of chicken nuggets, he gets apple slices and instead of apple juice, he gets water. (Honestly, if you're looking for something else to let go of in life, make it junk food.)

Benji also knows McDonovan's has reasonably tidy and – most importantly – private bathroom facilities. I pulled over onto the shoulder again and googled the nearest McDonovan's. It was in the town of Werribee, about a fifteen-minute detour off the freeway.

'Right! Okay!' Werribee it would be.

As we neared the exit ramp to Werribee I spotted a service station, shimmering like an oasis in the desert. I swung the car into the entrance, parked and ran inside, but the guy at the counter said they didn't have a toilet. When I was back behind the wheel Benji reminded me again how badly he needed to go.

Fifteen minutes later we pulled up at Werribee McDonald's and headed straight to the bathrooms. The first door I saw was a kids' dunny that had a change table inside. Perfect, I thought as I kicked it open with Benji in tow. We both took one look at the toilet, however, and felt instantly nauseous. Someone had missed badly. It was beyond disgusting and Benji got extremely upset.

'It's okay, buddy. There's another toilet,' I soothed as I quickly pulled him outside and closed the door to that house of horrors. 'Just hold on – we're nearly there.'

Next, I opened the door to the male toilet, took one step inside and slipped over, falling heavily on my backside in something wet with my hands outstretched. Someone had vomited all over the floor and now I was sitting in it. As I slumped there in shock, with cold sick soaking into the seat of my jeans, Benji – with whom I was now eye-to-eye – smiled.

'Dad?'

'Yes, mate?'

'I don't really need to go to the toilet. I was just joking.'

I didn't know whether to laugh or cry. Both would have been appropriate, I guess. After I cleaned myself up, Benji and I resumed the closing stages of our much-anticipated family holiday. I wish there was a photo of my face at that moment to perfectly capture the essence of it all.

As the Melbourne skyline came into view, my thoughts returned to Anita. Through the years that we will all remember for COVID-19 she'd helped me grow and learn so much, not only about myself, but about the human condition. I was grateful to her for helping me understand what I needed to let go of – that embarrassing laundry list of shame, expectation, control, perfection, ego, fear of failure and addiction to social media – habits and behaviours I'd clung on to for years and that were holding me back.

But as I neared home with the faint whiff of a stranger's vomit in my nostrils it was Anita's statement of the obvious that rang loudest in my ears: life has always been messy, and it probably always will be.

It's what we do when we are in that mess that counts.

ACKNOWLEDGEMENTS

Writing a book during lockdown while having two young kids who don't sleep might be the most resilient thing I have ever done!

This book would not have happened, however, without the love and support of some incredible people. I have no idea in what order to thank them all, so I'm just going to list them as they pop into my head.

First, to everyone who wrote to me after the publication of my first book, thank you. I had planned to get back to every one of you individually, until the sheer number of you made that impossible! Please know that your kind words and love inspired this book.

To my in-laws, Anne, Rob and Nick, who I love dearly. You did everything you could within the lockdown laws to

LET GO

help look after our kids so that I could find time and space to think and write. The relationship I have with the three of you is so special to me. I know not everyone gets to have this relationship with their in-laws, so I am extremely grateful.

To everyone in The Resilience Project team. I love you all very much and I cannot believe how lucky I am to work with you. While I often end up receiving the credit, you are the ones who managed to take our school program and curriculum to 320,000 kids around the country this year while I was busy writing this book. You are an exceptional group of people who inspire me every single day. In no order whatsoever, Laura, Helen, Kim, Antony, Peter, Belinda, Leah, Maddy, Elias, Rac, Ben, Dawn, Sarah, Alisha, Peter, Lael, Jeremy, Jack, Ashlee, Lisa and Beefy. You are the most humble and passionate group of people, and you have helped inspire millions around the country to feel happier.

A very special mention goes to our CEO, Ben Waterman. If COVID had happened four years ago, TRP wouldn't have survived. Because of you, Ben, we not only survived but thrived. And to Martin Heppell, our lead presenter. No one in the country is better at presenting to young people than you are. In fact, no one comes close. You are extraordinary at what you do. I love all that you do for us professionally, but in life it is the friendship I'm most grateful for. It is such an exciting privilege to call you my close friend.

To my WhatsApp group 'Big Hamstring Energy' (aka Kevin and Catriona), you gave me a very safe place to express how I was feeling at any given time throughout this last year, which was particularly selfless considering one of you was trying to focus on competing at the Olympics. You also help me run a lot faster. And that's important! I love you both.

To Puff and Dolly (sweaty eye guy!), your friendship has ensured I am the fittest and healthiest I have ever been, which has had an enormous impact on my writing. Love you both dearly.

To Ryan and Josh. Our little podcast is one of the most beautiful and authentic experiences of my life and has had a very big influence on the way this book has come together. You both make me so happy and while we say it multiple times a week anyway, I'll put it on paper and make it official, I love you both and I love our podcast.

To Ben Crowe, whose work has inspired me on so many levels. You have truly taught me how to accept myself for exactly who I am, without which this book wouldn't have happened.

To my psychologist, Anita, you have changed my life and I will be forever grateful.

To everyone who has given me permission to include their story in this book, thank you. By sharing your story, you will be helping so many people.

To my incredible team at Penguin Random House: Sophie, Craig, Rod and Kathryn. I received a lot of credit for the first book, which was lovely, but I couldn't help but feel guilty about receiving all the praise. I don't think people quite understand how much goes into a book from your end. To Sophie Ambrose, my publisher, I think you are a genius. Your expertise, focus, gentle guidance and compassionate outlook on the world have had a huge influence on both me and my writing. You receive nowhere near enough credit for what you do. You are amazing.

To Craig Henderson. Writing with you is one of the greatest joys I have ever known. I have learnt so much from you. My favourite part about the process of the first book was spending time in the surf together, followed by your home-cooked roast chicken. While COVID robbed us of the opportunity to connect like that again, it didn't hinder our ability to connect emotionally. You are such a beautiful person and I will never be able to thank you enough for both your brilliance and your friendship.

To my sister-in-law, Sophie, I am forever grateful for the influence you have had on our family. From the day Josh first introduced you to us, you have been a constant source of joy and energy. I am so lucky to have you in my life and I love you very much.

To Charlie, my busy, curious and active nephew. You have brought so much happiness into all of our lives. Your cousins are obsessed with you. And so are Penny and I. We will always be here for you, like a second family. I love you more than you will ever know, Charlie.

To Mum and Dad. I am who I am because of you. Your sacrifices, your unconditional love and your immense and ongoing support have made me who I am. If Benji and Elsie one day talk about me the way that I talk about both of you, I will know I have done my job as a parent. In writing this book I have spent countless hours reflecting on my childhood. It really was perfect. I wouldn't change a thing. Thank you for everything you have given me. I love you both too much to put into words.

The sibs, Georgia and Josh. Thank you for allowing me to share so many of our childhood stories. I know they will help so many people. Georgia, while you are on the other side of the world, I have never felt closer to you. I have wonderful memories of our childhood together. Thank you for allowing me to open both of my books with your truly inspiring story. I love you. Josh, the journey of parenting is one I am truly relishing the chance to share with you. I can't wait for our kids to grow up together. I love you.

Penny, there is absolutely no way known this book would have happened without you. How you have survived this year I will never, ever understand. You have endured 250-plus days in lockdown, with two kids who don't sleep and a husband trying to write a book. Amid all this, you have created your phenomenal website, 'So OCD', to help others living with OCD. Everything you do is about helping others, whether that's our family or the millions of people around the world who have OCD. I am so proud of you. I love you. Thank you for ensuring this book could happen.

Benji and Elsie, I love you more than anything in this world. On the rare occasion that you both allow me to cuddle you on the couch at the same time, in that moment I'm the happiest I've ever been. Whenever I found myself lacking energy or motivation while writing this book, I thought of you both and was instantly filled with the inspiration I needed to push on. Now, please, please learn to sleep. Oh, and thanks for not reading Chapter 4!

NOTES

CHAPTER 1: DEAR GEORGIA, TAKE TWO

1. Tangney, J. P., Stuewig, J., and Mashek, D. J. (2007), 'Moral emotions and moral behavior', *Annual Review of Psychology*, vol. 58, pp. 345–72
2. Tangney, J. P. (1995), 'Recent advances in the empirical study of shame and guilt', *American Behavioral Scientist*, vol. 38, no. 8, pp. 1132–45
3. Manson, Mark, 'The best way to resolve your shame', https://markmanson. net/shame
4. Okura, Lynn, 'Brené Brown on shame: "It cannot survive empathy"', HuffPost, 26 August 2013, www.huffpost.com/entry/brene-brown-shame_n_3807115
5. Manson, 'The best way to resolve your shame'

CHAPTER 3: THE BEAUTIFUL BREAKDOWN

1. 'Australia named among second most depressed countries in the world', Scimex, 31 March 2017, www.scimex.org/newsfeed/who-estimates-say-australian-is-the-most-depressed-country-in-the-western-pacific-region
2. 'Resilient Youth data definitive measure of mental health for Australians', Resilient Youth Australia, 13 September 2018, http://resilientyouth.org/blog/mental-health-data-australia

CHAPTER 5: A PAIN IN THE BUM

1. Brown, Brené, *Daring Greatly: How the courage to be vulnerable transforms the way we live, love, parent, and lead*, Penguin Life, London, 2016
2. Katie, Bryon, with Stephen Mitchell, *A Mind at Home With Itself: How asking four questions can free your mind, open your heart, and turn your world around*, HarperCollins, New York, 2017

CHAPTER 6: ONE (NOT SO) PERFECT DAY

1. Curran, Thomas, and Andrew P. Hill (2019), 'Perfectionism is increasing over time: A meta-analysis of birth cohort differences from 1989 to 2016' Psychological Bulletin, vol. 145, no. 4, pp. 410–29
2. Ruggeri, Amanda, 'The dangerous downsides of perfectionism', BBC Future, 21 February 2018, www.bbc.com/future/article/20180219-toxic-perfectionism-is-on-the-rise
3. Ferrari, Madeleine, Keong Yap, Nicole Scott, Danielle A. Einstein, and Joseph Ciarrochi, (2018), 'Self-compassion moderates the perfectionism and depression link in both adolescence and adulthood', *PLOS ONE*, vol. 13, no. 2

CHAPTER 8: TEACHING THE TEACHER

1. Usborne, Simon, 'How to get to a world without suicide', Mosaic, 31 July 2017, https://mosaicscience.com/story/zero-suicide-mental-health

CHAPTER 10: LIFE OF RYAN

1. Gable, Shelly L., Harry T. Reis, Emily A. Impett, and Evan R. Asher (2004), 'What do you do when things go right? The intrapersonal and interpersonal benefits of sharing positive events', *Journal of Personality snd Social Psychology*, vol. 87, no. 2, pp. 228–45

CHAPTER 11: GOING WITH THE FLOW

1. 'Your brain performs better when it slows down, with Steven Kotler', Big Think, 4 November 2014, https://bigthink.com/surprising-science/steven-kotler-flow-states
2. Csikszentmihalyi, Mihaly, *Flow: The psychology of happiness*, Rider Books, London, 2002, p. 74
3. Dietrich, Arne, *How Creativity Happens in the Brain*, Palgrave Macmillan, Basingstoke, Hampshire, 2015

CHAPTER 12: A FILE CALLED REGRET, TAKE TWO

1. Cunningham, Melissa, 'Trapped in the net: Are we all addicted to our smartphones?', *The Age*, 1 June 2019, www.theage.com.au/national/victoria/trapped-in-the-net-are-we-all-addicted-to-our-smartphones-20190531-p51t44.html

2. Richtel, Matt, 'Children's screen time has soared in the pandemic, alarming parents and researchers', *New York Times*, 17 January 2021, www.nytimes.com/2021/01/16/health/covid-kids-tech-use.html
3. O'Dea, S., 'Number of smartphones sold to end users worldwide from 2007 to 2021', Statista, 13 September 2021, www.statista.com/statistics/263437/global-smartphone-sales-to-end-users-since-2007

CHAPTER 14: LESSONS FROM MY DAD
1. As outlined by Ryan Holiday in *Ego Is the Enemy*, Profile Books, London, 2016

MENTAL HEALTH SUPPORT SERVICES

Adult

Lifeline: 13 11 14
lifeline.org.au

Suicide Call Back Service: 1300 659 467
suicidecallbackservice.org.au

Beyond Blue: 1300 22 4636
beyondblue.org.au

MensLine Australia: 1300 78 99 78
mensline.org.au

Youth

Kids Helpline: 1800 55 1800
kidshelpline.com.au

headspace: 1800 650 890
headspace.org.au

ReachOut: au.reachout.com

Other resources

Life in Mind (suicide prevention portal):
lifeinmindaustralia.com.au

Head to Health (mental health portal): headtohealth.gov.au

SANE (online forums): sane.org

ABOUT THE AUTHOR

Hugh van Cuylenburg has been working in education for more than seventeen years, teaching both primary and secondary in a range of educational settings. He has completed postgraduate studies looking at resilience and wellbeing, and has developed and facilitated programs for more than 1500 schools Australia-wide.

In 2015, the National Rugby League asked Hugh to design and implement a series of comprehensive workshops at every single club in the competition. Since then, he has worked with the Australian cricket team, the Australian netball team, the Australian women's soccer team, the Australian women's rugby league team, ten AFL teams, the Australian Olympic Committee and every soccer team in the A-League. Beyond the team environment, Hugh has worked one-on-one with individuals such as Steve Smith, Billy Slater and Dustin Martin.

Outside of schools and elite sport, Hugh has presented to hundreds of corporate organisations as a keynote speaker, and for three years running his national speaking tour has sold out. He is also co-host of the popular podcast *The Imperfects*.